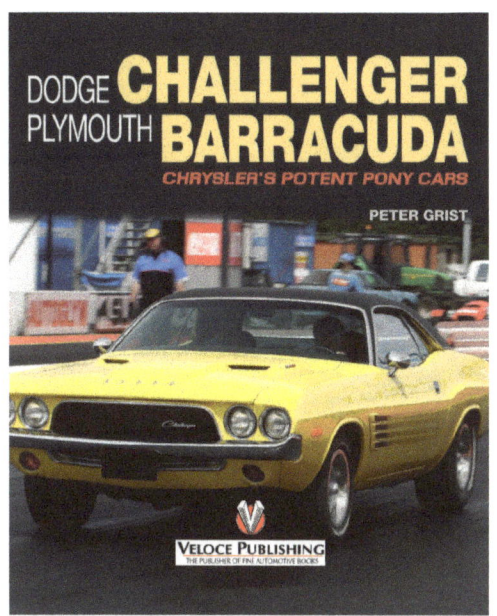

Other great books from Veloce –

Chrysler 300 – America's Most Powerful Car 2nd Edition (Ackerson)
Dodge Charger – Enduring Thunder (Ackerson)
Dodge Dynamite! (Grist)
Ford F100/F150 Pick-up 1948-1996 (Ackerson)
Ford F150 Pick-up 1997-2005 (Ackerson)
Ford Midsize Muscle – Fairlane, Torino & Ranchero (Cranswick)
Ford Small Block V8 Racing Engines 1962-1970 – The Essential Source Book (Hammill)
Ford Thunderbird From 1954, The Book of the (Long)
N.A.R.T. – A concise history of the North American Racing Team 1957 to 1983 (O'Neil)
Northeast American Sports Car Races 1950-1959 (O'Neil)
Pontiac Firebird – New 3rd Edition (Cranswick)
PT Cruiser – Chrysler's classic design for a modern age (Ackerson)
Virgil Exner – Visioneer (Grist)

www.veloce.co.uk

First published in April 2007, paperback edition printed March 2017 by Veloce Publishing Limited, Veloce House, Parkway Farm Business Park, Poundbury, Dorchester, Dorset DT1 3AR, England. Phone 01305 260068/fax 01305 268864/e-mail info@veloce.co.uk/web www.veloce.co.uk or www.velocebooks.com.
ISBN: 978-1-787110-94-6/UPC: 6-36847-01094-2
© Pete Grist and Veloce Publishing 2007 & 2017. All rights reserved. With the exception of quoting brief passages for the purpose of review, no part of this publication may be recorded, reproduced or transmitted by any means, including photocopying, without the written permission of Veloce Publishing Ltd. Throughout this book logos, model names and designations, etc, have been used for the purposes of identification, illustration and decoration. Such names are the property of the trademark holder as this is not an official publication.
Readers with ideas for automotive books, or books on other transport or related hobby subjects, are invited to write to the editorial director of Veloce Publishing at the above address.
British Library Cataloguing in Publication Data – A catalogue record for this book is available from the British Library. Typesetting, design and page make-up all by Veloce Publishing Ltd on Apple Mac. Printed and Bound by CPI Group (UK) Ltd, Croydon, CR04YY.

DODGE CHALLENGER
PLYMOUTH BARRACUDA

CHRYSLER'S POTENT PONY CARS

PETER GRIST

VELOCE PUBLISHING
THE PUBLISHER OF FINE AUTOMOTIVE BOOKS

For John E Herlitz
30 December 1942–24 March 2008

Contents

Acknowledgments..5
Introduction...6
1. Valiant beginnings...8
    The big fish – 1964 Barracuda...15
    The frantic fish...32
2. Second generation 1967-1969..37
    1968 The beat goes on...49
    Hemi Barracuda Super Stock..55
    1969 The 'Cuda swims in..59
    Aquatic savage...66
3. No shrinking violet – 1970...71
    1970 Barracuda..82
    'Cuda...85
    1970 Challenger...90
4. The ultimate pony car – 1971...131
    Flash fish: 1971 Barracuda..132
    1971 Challenger...140
5. Scaling down – 1972-1974...150
    1972 Barracuda..155
    1972 Challenger...159
    1973 Off the hook..167
    1974 The final catch...172
6. The one that got away..177
Index..191

Acknowledgments

With a book on such a well loved subject as Chrysler's momentous pony cars, it was important for me to get as much information from as many respected sources as possible, so I have tried to talk to as many people as I could that actually had a hand in creating these wonderful cars. You can't get better than first-hand evidence. Regardless, there will always be controversy or differences of opinion from people having different memories. Where there is doubt I have gone with the general consensus.

Sadly, designer John Herlitz died just before work on this project started, which is why it is dedicated to him. But so many others that had a hand in creating the Plymouth Barracuda and Dodge Challenger have also passed on, some destined never to have their work recognized. I hope this book in some way redresses the balance and gives credit to some of those responsible for creating the cars of our dreams. Thankfully, some of the key players are still with us, strong, fit and healthy, and I could not have done this book without their help, so I would like to thank John Samsen, Milt Antonick, Jeff Godshall and Bob Ackerman for their time and patience. Automobile enthusiast Brett Snyder deserves a special mention, along with his superb Andrew F Johnson Gallery of Automotive Concept & Illustration Art, a stunning website that deserves a look! find it at www.andrewfjohnsongallery.com

Thanks to photographer Marc Rozman who found many images that I couldn't, Brandt Rosenbusch at the Chrysler archives for coming up trumps yet again, Tony Oksien for images and the history on his Barracuda, James and Roydon Mitchell for letting me snap their 1972 Barracuda, Peter Wiseman for his 1970 Challenger, Jim Wilson for both his Challenger and 'Cuda, Grahame Bloomfield for his 1973 340, David Fogg for images of his 1970 AAR 'Cuda and David Castine for images of his lovely 1970 'Cuda 440. Brad Barrie gave me lots of help with the Savage GT history and images of his car. Barry Washington and David Robson took the time to proofread the manuscript for me and give valuable input, while Barry also helped out with some rare images and David helped with statistics. Thank you to the guys at the Dodge Challenger message board and the Mopar Muscle Association, and to Dean Ackerman for help with his father's sketches. Rod Grainger at Veloce Publishing deserves a mention for having faith in my abilities, and finally, thanks to my ever-patient wife Catherine, who not only proofreads for me but puts up with my tap-tapping at the computer until the wee small hours. Thank you all.

I would like to recommend some additional reading that was also of help when writing this book.

Riding The Roller Coaster Hyde, Charles K Wayne, State University Press

Barracuda & Challenger Color History Zazarine, Paul C, Motorbooks International

Chrysler Chronicles Flammang, James M, Publications International.

Mighty Mopars 1960-1974 Young, Anthony, Motorbooks International.

Standard Catalogue of Chrysler 1924-1990 Lee, John, Krause Publications.

Peter Grist
Southampton, UK

Introduction

The term 'pony cars' originates from the equestrian sounding and ever popular Ford Mustang, the quintessential early muscle car. Surely though, this small but much coveted group within the consumer market should have been called 'fishy cars' ...

The Plymouth division of Chrysler beat Ford to the dealerships by a clear two weeks when it introduced its Barracuda on April 1, 1964. American Motors Corporation (AMC) released the similarly fastback-styled Marlin on March 1 the following year, which in turn had been based on yet another aquatically-named concept, the Rambler Tarpon of 1964. However, with its unique mix of performance, light weight and smart design, the Mustang managed to outsell the competition by a large margin. It is unclear who coined the term pony car in the mid-sixties, although it sounds dramatically better than the alternative; but whatever name is used, the story of Chrysler's pony cars starts long before the introduction of the Mustang. In fact, all pony cars can thank Chevrolet for their existence.

By 1960, all of the Big Three and some of the smaller auto manufacturers were building compact cars, and in the following three years each maker would try and define, in its own inimitable way, the purpose and market for the new cars. Traditionally, car makers avoid production of small cars, because the lower price tag greatly affects the profit margin of each unit. To overcome this, manufacturers pandered to the wants of the buyers by adding accessories and ever more options. The best of these was the Chevy Corvair Monza Spyder. Because of its rear-engined configuration the Monza was never available with a V8, but what it did offer in its diminutive body was sporty European styling, and a sports interior based around separate bucket seats. Introduced in mid-1962 and powered by a nippy 150bhp, turbocharged, aluminium, air-cooled 140in^3 (2.3 L) flat-6 engine, the Spyder coupes and convertibles expanded on the success of the basic Corvair. With improved suspension, an even more powerful engine for the following year, and a host of accessories thrown in, sales increased in what had become a dwindling market.

The sales figures were not lost on Ford boss Lee Iacocca, who also noted the young, educated buyers this car was attracting, including an ever increasing amount of young women. Iacocca saw the opportunity to tempt those buyers away from Chevrolet with something the Monza couldn't offer: V8 power! In 1961 Ford replied to the Corvair with the Falcon-based Futura, and mid-way through 1963 it released the vivacious Futura Sprint. The Sprint offered a 164bhp 260in^3 V8 along with a sporty hardtop or convertible, bucket seats, a 6000rpm tachometer and a manual floor shifted 4-speed transmission. It was sporty, but it was really just a stop-gap, as Iacocca had a plan – it was called the Ford Mustang.

Using a reskinned Ford Falcon base, the Ford design team of Joe Oros, David Ash and Gale Halderman came up with a long hood/short deck body that wrapped around a peppy 101bhp straight-six – also taken from the Falcon – or an optional 260in^3 Challenger engine. The success of the Mustang surprised the entire auto industry, including Iacocca. In its first four months of production, the new Ford sold a staggering 126,538 units compared to 214,483 total year sales for the Monza, and by the beginning of 1966, it had sold well over 1 million. So it was Chevrolet's Monza that was the catalyst for the creation of the pony car market, but let's look at what Chrysler used for bait when it went fishing for those same young professional buyers.

The Corvair Monza was the catalyst for all pony cars. Individual looks with sporty handling and a plethora of options for the buyer made this an attractive proposition.

Although Ralph Nader had taken a shot at the early Corvair in his book *Unsafe At Any Speed,* the cars were developed over the following years, losing any shortcomings they may have had. This is a 1966 Monza and shows why the Mustang would go on and outsell it, the Corvair was rear-engined and not able to accommodate a V8 engine.

1

Valiant beginnings

In the mid 1950s, there were strong signs of a change in consumer attitudes. The public was saying that it wanted smaller automobiles, especially when the recession took hold in 1958. To underline this, cars like the small VW Beetle and other foreign imports were selling well, along with the home-grown AMC Rambler, so Chrysler announced that it would finally build its first compact. Ford and GM were ahead of the game already, with work on their Falcon and Corvair well under way. Chrysler bosses still dragged their collective corporate feet until it was obvious even to them that a sea change in taste was developing. They turned to Chrysler's vice president of design, Virgil M Exner Snr, for a response.

Exner had come from a long and successful tenure as design chief at Studebaker in South Bend, Indiana, and was hired into Chrysler in 1949 by the then corporate president K T Keller. Exner set to work creating a series of exciting idea, or concept, cars that helped lift the depression hanging over the company at that time. The cars also helped Keller get financial backing from investors so that he could turn around the fortunes of the struggling automotive giant.

So successful were these early idea cars that Keller gave Exner responsibility for all car production design from 1954 onwards, his biggest successes coming in 1955 and 1957 with the finned Forward Look vehicles. As a reward for his success Exner was promoted to the board, becoming the first VP of design at Chrysler.

Exner had been working on a classically styled, long hood/short deck compact car for some time, and by late 1959 the car was ready for release. The Valiant project gave Exner his first true opportunity to utilise his planned fuselage design, and attempt to get side glass as flush to the door panels as possible, and would also be the precursor to the platform type of design method, where body and chassis engineers worked alongside stylists to produce a complete package. Although Exner had been responsible for the Chrysler Corporation's turnaround in the mid-fifties with his legendary high-finned designs, many critics wrongly assumed Exner was a one trick pony. He gave Chrysler a huge success with the Valiant, and to the many pundits who expected another high-finned, big-engined car, Chrysler's new compact was staggeringly different.

Although the Chrysler Corporation had toyed with the idea of building a compact as early as 1936 with its Star Car and the later Interceptor (1941) and Cadet (1947), a name also used by Chevrolet for one of its postwar compact designs – some of which got as far as the prototype stage – Chrysler bosses still believed the buying public did not want small, economical vehicles, but rather larger, more comfortable cars. They actively held onto this misapprehension until the closing stages of the 1950s, when even the most stubborn corporate executives had to admit that there was a market for smaller cars in North America.

By May of 1958, Chrysler's then president, Tex Colbert, had set up the Small Car Study Program, headed by Chrysler chief engineer Harry Chesebrough, to develop a car ready for release in 1962, coded Project A901. Exner, still not ready to forget about the demise of his two-seater Falcon idea cars of 1955, desperately wanted this new project to become a reality. The Chrysler Falcon had been a sports car that would have given the Ford Thunderbird and Chevrolet Corvette a run for their money, but Chrysler executives decided not to put the attractive roadster into production.

Shortly after, Chrysler bosses learned that Ford and General Motors were both planning to launch

1955 Chrysler Falcon. This was Chrysler styling Vice-President Virgil M Exner's answer to Ford's Thunderbird and Chevrolet's Corvette. Larger than both of the aforementioned sports cars, the Falcon was a Hemi-powered, two-seat sports roadster built using unit construction with an integral, cellular platform frame. Three of these cars were produced in 1955, colored red, blue and black, with Exner keeping the black one as personal transportation for many years.

their compacts for the 1960 model year. This really put the cat amongst the pigeons, and the planning group began to bicker amongst themselves as to what was to be done. The original plan of building a four-seater that could return 25 to 30mpg and sell for as little as $1850 soon fell by the wayside. In a product planning meeting held on the 8th July 1958, Chesebrough and Exner showed two full-size clay models, one with a wheelbase of 106in and the other with a 103in base, both wearing Falcon nameplates. Almost immediately, it became evident that the 106in model was the only viable option. Changes had been made to the specifications that now asked for seating for six adults, weight had increased by 400lb over the initial recommendation, and fuel economy had dropped significantly down to 22mpg. The committee gave the go ahead for the new car to be developed for production for 1960.

Chrysler sent teams of designers, engineers and marketing people to Europe to study compact cars, leading eventually to the company's investment in Simca and its decision to create an American-built compact car. By the end of July, a team of more than two hundred engineers and designers had moved into 403 Midland Avenue, in the centre of Chrysler's Detroit complex, and then worked in complete secrecy to develop the new car. The development project was code-named Falcon. "Exner was intensely involved in the development

Dodge Challenger & Plymouth Barracuda

1960 Chrysler Valiant. Developed through 1959 in complete secrecy, the Valiant was Chrysler's answer to Ford's Falcon and the Chevy Corvair. This quirky little car was a sales success for Chrysler, and oddly, it predicted where design Vice-President Virgil Exner was going with his styling. Odd because he introduced styling cues on the low-priced Valiant that he wanted to float up to the more expensive models, instead of starting at the top and watering down the designs to the cheaper offerings. The Valiant initially sold as a separate marque, only becoming a Plymouth sub-series in 1961. Offered in two lines, the base V-100 and more luxurious V-200, the V-200 was easily identified by the stainless steel strip that ran from behind the front wheel opening to the rear of the car. The car was powered by an all new 170.9in^3 slant six that offered frugal use of fuel, but allowed for performance options to be fitted. With the Hyper Pak option, horsepower rose from 101 to 148.

of the Valiant," recalls Bill Brownlie, a designer at Chrysler. "He wanted an elegant look as opposed to cheap, thus the six-window roof and Ferrari mouth."

Exner rejected the idea of simply scaling down a large car to create a small one for the North American market. His goal was to create a smaller, lighter car without sacrificing passenger and luggage space. Other Chrysler employees not involved in the project were told that the team were working on a special defence contract, which was not unusual at Chrysler.

During the Falcon project, more than 20 prototypes

Valiant beginnings

were built and 57 experimental engines operated for 750 million test miles. By August 1959, the job was complete, with the first car rolling off the production line just one month later. Throughout its development, the new compact continued to be called the Falcon, after Exner's previous idea car from 1955, but Henry Ford II wanted the name for the Ford Motor Company's new compact. Because Chrysler had used the name on its idea cars, Henry Ford approached Chrysler president Tex Colbert and asked if he could have the name. Not wanting to let Ford know that he had an all-new car waiting in the wings, Colbert's first instinct was to say yes to the request. Exner's son, Virgil Exner Junior states that Tex approached his father to ask how he felt about giving Ford the name. Reluctantly, the VP for design replied, "Well, I guess they do us some favours once in a while and we do them some favours, so that's ok." But Junior also says that his father came up with the replacement name of Valiant. "Back in those days, marketing, advertising and design came up with the names of the cars. Father always liked Prince Valiant, the comic strip. It was one of his favourite comic strips because of how well it was drawn by the artist Hal Foster. So he decided it would be neat to have Valiant as the name of the car." This goes against archive records that suggest Chrysler conducted extensive polling of customers, asking them to come up with a name for the new car. From over two thousand suggestions from customers in 15 American cities, a short list was reduced to just five names including Columbia and Liberty, with Valiant coming out on top.

However it was named, the Valiant arrived in dealerships in October 1959 as a 1960 model, interestingly as a marque of its own, and it was not until 1961 that it became a Plymouth in America (although it became a Chrysler in export markets, except for Canada where it remained its own marque, being sold by both Plymouth and Dodge dealers). The cars, all built at the Dodge plant in St Louis, Missouri, were all four-door sedans and featured typical Exner touches that were inspired by European styles: the radiator sized front grille, open wheel arches, sports-deck trunk lid, ridged fenders, a squared-off greenhouse and classic long-nose and short rear-deck proportions. The distinct Valiant body style was set using crisp blade-like lines on the front fenders that were matched at the rear, culminating in oval shaped taillights. Exner wanted to see a continuous curve from the roof down to the sills, which required thinner doors and almost flush window-to-door fitment. Odd-looking perhaps, but they were incredibly successful.

Priced between the Falcon and Corvair, out of the three, the Valiant was by far the best engineered, the best handling and the quickest, but high sales of 180,000 units in its first year could not match Ford's 417,000 Falcons, or even the 253,268 Corvairs sold by Chevrolet. The Valiant was fitted with a radical new 170in^3 slant six that gave 101bhp in its basic form. The slant six was named because it canted to the right, allowing for a much lower hood design. This was fitted to a 3-speed manual gearbox as standard or as a cost option, the new smaller Torqueflite 904 automatic gearbox. This lighter box was made from aluminium, saving a whopping 60lb of weight, and was activated by Chrysler's famous push-button changer. This box also featured the first internal transmission parking on the main shaft fitted to a ChryCo passenger car. Mechanical fingers engaged the shaft, preventing it from turning. They were actuated by the driver using a lever situated next to push buttons for the Torqueflite to the left of the steering wheel on the dash.

Underneath the Uni-body shell there was torsion bar front suspension and rear leaf springs. The Valiant was the first with an alternating electrical system instead of the more traditional direct current generator. The whole body of the car underwent a seven-dip rust proofing sequence before receiving two coats of 'Lustre-bond' enamel paint.

The Valiant was a big hit for Chrysler in an otherwise glum year, but even more overlooked than its sales success was its amazing achievement at the track; the mid-season release of a hyper-package boosted horsepower up to 148bhp, giving racers power aplenty. The package consisted of a long, tuned ram intake manifold, 4-barrel carb and dual-exhaust manifolds. With tweaking, engineers were able to squeeze up to 185bhp from some race engines. The results were incredible; on the 31st January 1960, NASCAR held its inaugural 'Compact car division' road race in conjunction with the Daytona 500. Led by Lee Petty, the seven Valiants entered took the first seven places across the line in the ten lap preliminary race, then three Valiants

Dodge Challenger & Plymouth Barracuda

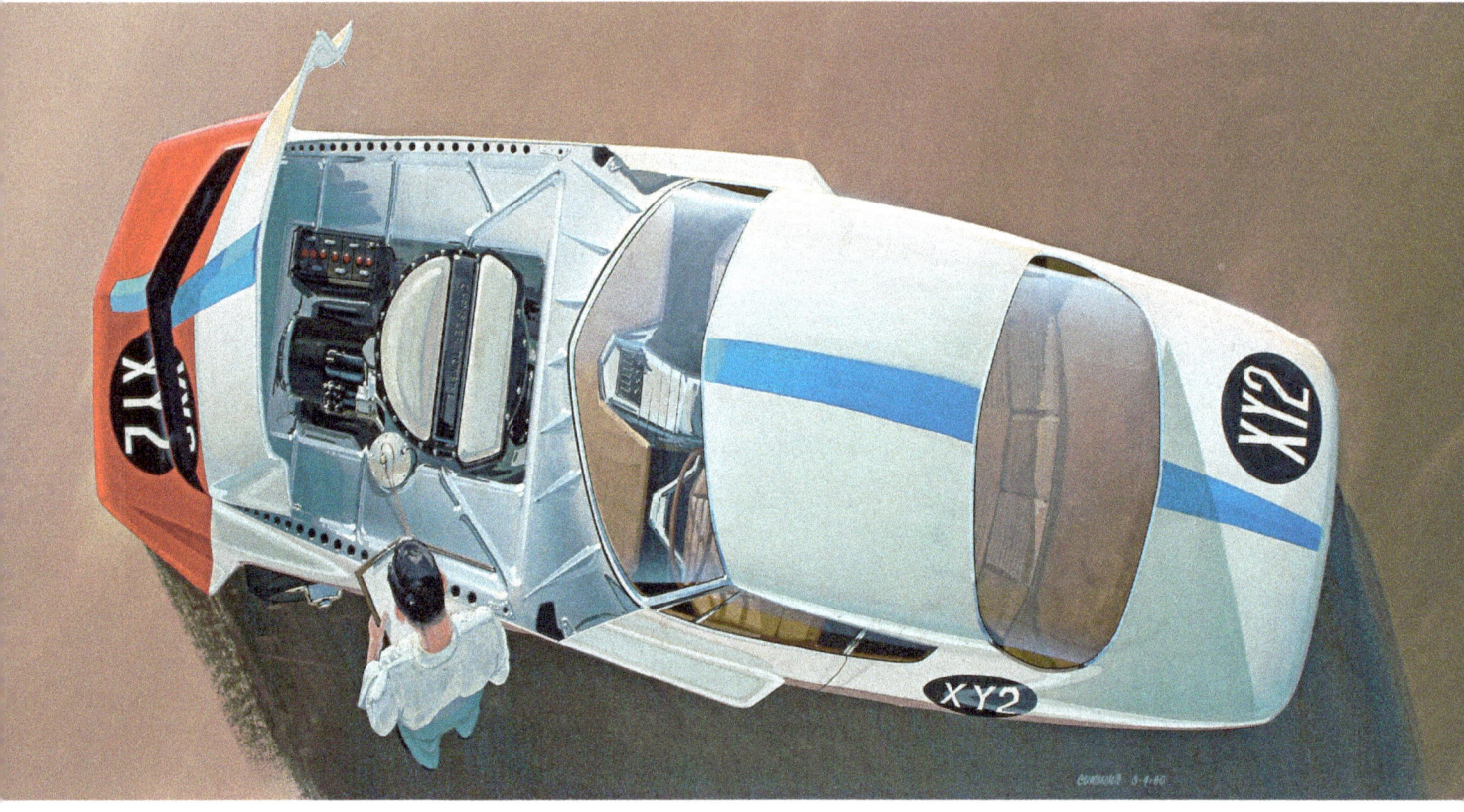

XY2. This detailed drawing of a Chrysler Turbine-powered race car was drawn by Dave Cummins in 1960. With its large rear greenhouse area, this was one of the earliest incarnations of a fastback at Chrysler and would eventually lead to the 1964 Barracuda. (Courtesy Hampton Wayt)

driven by Marvin Panch, Roy Schecter and Larry Frank finished 1st, 2nd and 3rd in the main twenty lap race in front of a televised audience sponsored by Chevrolet. They reached speeds of 122mph, beating European imports and V8 models! When the Valiant did the same thing the following year, NASCAR cancelled the series.

During the same period the Valiant also won the Mobil Fuel Economy Challenge, providing an interesting mix of both fuel economy and performance capabilities in a small car. Success for the gutsy little car in the United States and Canada soon spread to other Chrysler strongholds around the globe including Australia, the United Kingdom, South Africa, New Zealand and other international markets. Over time, the Valiant's reputation for distinctive design, solid engineering and dependability would quickly become legend.

Exner left Chrysler in 1962 in a cloud of controversy and was replaced by Ford designer Elwood Engle. Engle had worked on various projects at Ford and had been responsible for the design of the 1961 Lincoln. His employment at Chrysler would mean a long period for the company in a design wilderness where slab-sided, austere behemoths would become commonplace for its standard production cars. Although Engle was given credit for the curvaceous and more popular 1963 Valiant redesign, the lines were drawn by Plymouth stylists while still under Exner's guidance. The only changes made were to the rear panels which initially swept downwards at the back, but the new Chrysler President, Lyn Townsend, disliked them a great deal and ordered that the panels finish in a more traditional straight line. This platform was the basis for the first Barracuda, but had the potential for being a tricky job.

VALIANT BEGINNINGS

Plymouth Super Sport. This was how Chrysler executives saw the first Super Sport. The full-size clay model was double-sided; the right side wore a graceful C-pillar that kicked up at the flank and a traditional door with curved side glass, while the left side of the car had a more radical wrap-around rear screen and a longer door that cut higher into the roof. The rear end wore two similar but not identical versions of the fresh-looking horizontal fins. This car spawned a complete sequence of designs called the S series due for introduction in 1962, but they were downsized, ruining the delicate proportions needed to make the designs work. It was partly inspirational in the design of the Barracuda.

The use of unit body construction, introduced on the Valiant in 1959 and accepted across the corporation (except for Imperial) by 1961, was to reduce the effects of poor quality control issues suffered in 1957 and '58. The lack of a more traditional body on chassis was a major drawback when designing a new 'face-lift' car to fit around an existing monocoque fabrication.

When the DeSoto studio closed in 1959, most of the stylists from that studio moved over to Plymouth. Designer John Samsen, who had been hired by Virgil Exner in 1955, went from the DeSoto studio over to the Imperial studio. There he worked on ornamentation and taillamps for the '62 Imperial for less than a year before another reorganisation found him in the new Valiant/Lancer studio headed by Dick Macadam.

John had come from the Ford Exterior studio where he had worked since 1952 on projects like the first Thunderbird, concepts and the 1957 production cars. He remembers what it was like to work for Chrysler then: "I didn't like the working conditions in the Ford exterior studio; they demanded extreme pressure to produce, and many overtime hours. When I arrived at Chrysler I was assigned to the DeSoto Studio. I met the manager Dick Baird, assistant Jack Kennets and chief stylist Tom Bannister. There were half a dozen stylists in the studio, plus an illustrator and a tech man. I was amazed at how different it was from Ford exterior studio. I was given supplies and assigned a drawing board and left to my own devices. No one was working overtime, and when the manager was out and their sketching for the day was finished, the designers actually played games like sailing roles of masking tape, frisbee style, and spearing them mid air with T squares. We also had batting practice using sticks from drawing board covers as bats and pitching rolled up balls of masking tape. Well I stayed at my drawing board that first day doing sketches while the others played, but as working didn't seem to make any difference I joined in the games next day. It was so much more relaxed than Ford."

A further reorganisation in 1961 created a new Plymouth team, made up of Don Kopka as studio manager, Gerry Thorley assistant manager, and Milt Antonik, Dave Cummins, Bill Shannon, Irv Ritchie, Fred Schimmel, Pete Loda, Neil Walling, Bob Gale and John (Dick) Samsen. These men made up the collective that produced the curvy lines of the next incarnation, with the amazing talents of Bill Lucas as illustrator. Dodge, of course, created its own interpretation of the new look with the Valiant-based Lancer/Dart, and initially they were also designed in the Plymouth studio by the same team, alongside the Valiant, although Dodge stylists would take over the work in future years.

Above: From the time of its introduction at the New York World Fair, the Ford Mustang was available in hardtop, fastback and convertible forms. Sales far outstripped production, leading some dealers to auction their stock to the highest bidders. Shown here is a 1965 convertible.

1964 Barracuda. This factory photo shows the rear three-quarter view and emphasises the European look of the car. The Valiant badge is clearly seen on the right side of the rear valance as are the 100 series Valiant taillights. (Courtesy Chrysler Historical Dept)

THE BIG FISH – 1964 BARRACUDA

The design for a new fastback automobile was unusual in that the idea was created in the design studio, not from a suggestion from the sales, marketing or production departments, as was the norm. It was on the slightly longer '63 Valiant that stylist Irv Ritchie based his idea of a radical new fastback design, called the Barracuda, in 1962. He had always liked fastback cars like the popular Oldsmobile, Buicks, and Pontiacs from the late 1940s which, in turn, had been replaced by 'hardtop convertibles.' He had also seen the clay models and designs for the ill-fated 'S' series of cars planned for introduction in 1962, one of which was a fastback layout. He was additionally inspired by the 1953 Studebaker Coupe and 1962 Avanti.

Along with others within the automobile community, Ritchie was well aware of the worst kept secret of the time – Ford's planned new compact sports car based on the Falcon running gear – so he began to sketch fastback versions of the Valiant. The fastback design has always been considered sporty, but glass size limitations have always compromised visibility, and give the unwanted side effect of interior heat build-up. But what if a large, tinted-glass section could overcome these obstacles? Ritchie even went as far as producing a full-size drawing of the roofline and rear-end ghosted over a Valiant seating drawing, to prove the design was feasible. Plymouth styling executives saw the idea and became interested in taking it further, and persuaded Joe Sturm, head of Chrysler Product Planning to allow a design study on a full-size clay model.

As always, a very limited budget was on offer to create a totally new model, but executives wanted a piece of this quickly developing, but under represented part of the market, hoping to catch some of the sales being netted by the Chevrolet Monza. Plymouth engineers and designers looked to Irv Ritchie's idea for the Valiant from which they might build a sporty car of their own. From information that had been acquired from many sources, including several private investigation companies, Chrysler

1964 Barracuda full-size clay. This shot was taken in the Plymouth studio in April of 1963 and shows how close to the donor Valiant the Barracuda would be. The lake-style side pipes were abandoned before production, while in this photo it looks like the taillights are yet to be decided upon. They would eventually come from the 100 series Valiant. (Courtesy Chrysler Historical Dept)

Dodge Challenger & Plymouth Barracuda

Seen in many publications of the time, this is the best remembered Barracuda advert from its introduction midway through 1964.

knew that Ford was working on a wheelbase of about 108 inches. It was also aware that the car would have a 6-cylinder engine with a small V8 offered as an option. Transmission choices were assumed to be a standard fully synchronized 3-speed manual, a 4-speed manual and two automatic transmission choices of Ford-O-Matic or Cruise-O-Matic. Buyer convenience items would include power steering, disc brakes, radio, and perhaps even air conditioning. Chrysler was aware that the planned Ford car was to be built on the lowly Falcon chassis, utilising Falcon drivetrain components including its suspension, brakes and wheels. "The industry was rife with rumours of Ford's new Mustang," remembers Gene Weiss, retired Chrysler-Plymouth and Dodge product planning executive. "But the extent of how changed the Mustang was from the Falcon was not learned until it was too late, from a tooling standpoint, to do as much."

It is easy to see how Sturm was quickly convinced that a Valiant-based design was the way to match or even beat Ford to the release of a new sporty compact car. Designer John Samsen told me, "Ritchie and I were assigned to do design concept sketches of a fastback Valiant. I liked reverse-slant 'C-pillars' and large backlights, so that is what I presented. I was happy when I was chosen to direct the clay modelling of my design over Ritchie's. I'm sure Ritchie was disappointed that he did not get to direct the clay work, but he was always given credit for the initial concept. Engineering demanded large external hinges for the little trunk, so I designed the wide chrome band on the top of the deck lid to disguise the hinges. I was not happy with this as I preferred less chrome on cars. I did the hands-on design of the roof, backlight, and rear deck. Dave Cummins created the front grille. Most of the executives liked the car's

Valiant beginnings

Here is the simple and well laid out dash for the new car. The giveaway push-button actuator on the left identifies this as the 1964 Barracuda. The following year saw the transmission selector moved to the steering column or floor mounted, depending on which transmission was ordered. (Courtesy Chrysler Historical Dept)

design and decided to put it into production. The Plymouth division people came up with the name 'Panda' for the car, and when we designers made a fuss, told us to suggest names. My list of names included 'Barracuda,' and it was chosen." The actual Barracuda ornament first introduced on the 1966 models was designed by Plymouth stylist Milton (Milt) J Antonick fresh from his tenure at Studebaker, and was an instant success with everyone who saw it. It remained in use until the 1970 model year.

In essence, the first Barracuda was a Plymouth 'A-body' Valiant two-door coupe with a new fastback roof, a huge wraparound glass rear window, bucket seats and some sporty decoration. It was built on the Valiant assembly line in St Louis, and in its inaugural year was badged as the Plymouth Valiant Barracuda (body code V89), sharing all sheet metal forward of the firewall and below the beltline. Coded V89, it was introduced as a sub-model of Valiant's top range Signet line, and even on the owner's handbook was described as a Valiant Barracuda. At the front of the car it used a spiced up grille from the Valiant 100 series, but had large chrome surrounds, and also held two large side/turn signal lights nearer the central mesh section. The rear lights were also taken from the base 100 series Valiant.

For the Dodge division, while it had various performance versions of the Lancer compact (a twin sister to the Valiant) it didn't get, and didn't want, the fastback body in any form. That huge,

Two views of the rear seating and cargo area. With the rear seats folded flat a huge amount of space was available. The designer that gave the car its fishy name, John Samsen, owned an early Barracuda. "I placed an order with a Detroit dealer and took delivery of a silver Barracuda which I was quite happy with. On a trip to New England and the NY World Fair, I folded the rear seat and slept under the glass bubble several times. There was plenty of space in there." (Courtesy Chrysler Historical Dept)

The 1964 trunk offered a 7ft-long loading space when the rear seats were folded down, and 5.7ft when in the upright position. (Courtesy Chrysler Historical Dept)

tinted, compound-curve glassed area did cause problems through its development. With its enviable name for forward thinking work, the Pittsburgh Plate Glass Company (PPG) was chosen to make the glass backlight. Measuring in at 14.4ft square, it was the largest single piece of glass ever to be used on a car up to that point, and the production journey wasn't trouble-free. Chrysler produced clear plastic backlights and molds that PPG could use as a template to experiment with, but PPG found they were unable to hold the flat shape featured on the model and the plastic guide, and early production backlights had more of a bubble effect near the centre line. It was produced using the 'sag method' as opposed to the more expensive pressed glass. Advances in technology improved later models, but still never quite matched John Samsen's intended design shape.

Artwork from the time for ads and brochures was touched up to hide the bulbous look most

VALIANT BEGINNINGS

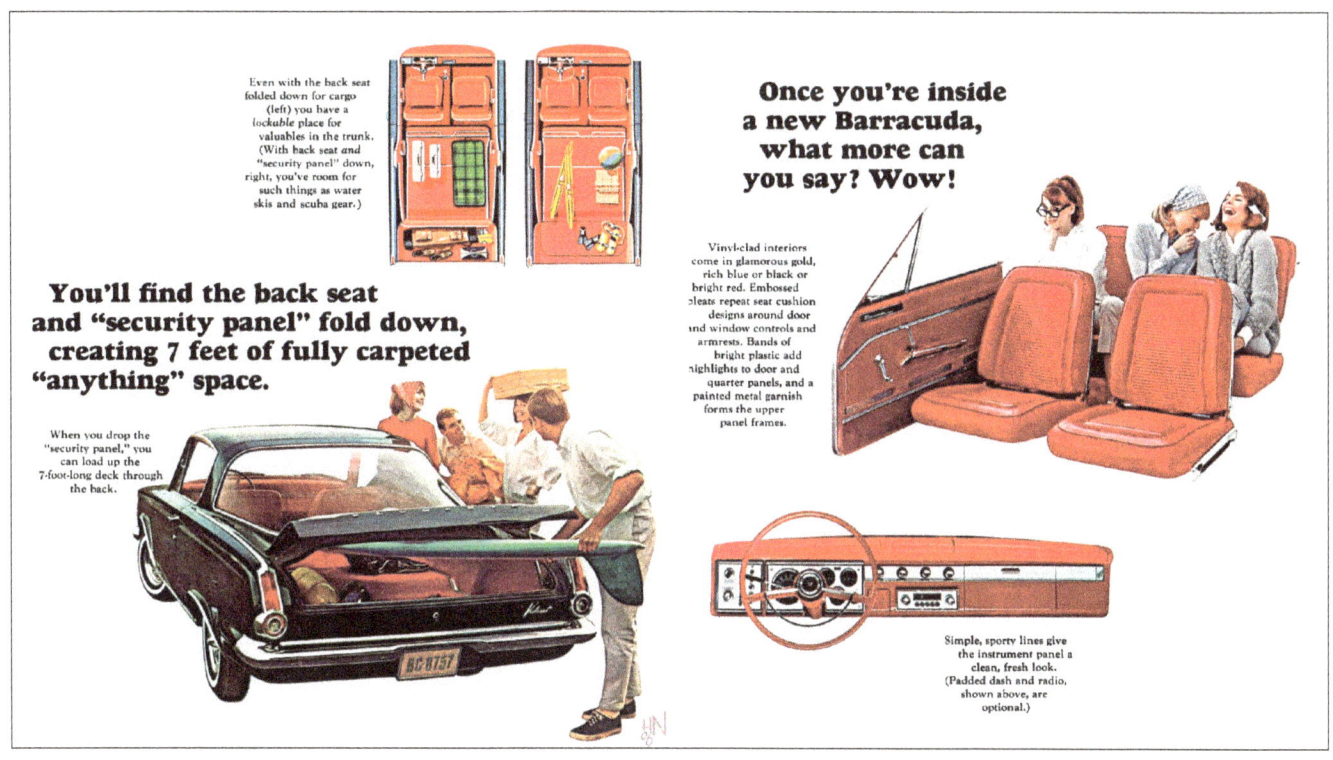

Part of the first Barracuda brochure produced. Emphasis was on utility, not performance, although the 273 V8 gets a mention.

notable in silhouette. The fastback design was more than just sporty looks; it made the car much more practical. Visibility was greatly enhanced, but of course it was the massive trunk space, increased dramatically when the rear seats were folded flat – an unusual occurrence in Detroit at that time – that allowed for cargo up to 7ft long, great for fishermen and skiers alike. A chrome bar attached to the back of the rear seats separated the carpeted trunk area from the front low-backed bucket seats, preventing forward motion of the cargo into the cockpit when the seats were folded down. If that wasn't enough space, there was another, smaller, lockable trunk hidden away under the carpet. The rest of the interior was fully carpeted, too, and complemented the plush ribbed padded bucket seats and matching trim panels. The vinyl trim came in four colors: P4B Blue, P4R Red, P4Y Gold and P4X Black.

The instrument panel was simplistic but easy to use. A large round dial held the speedometer and mileage counter on the left of the column, with three smaller dials to the right that held the fuel and oil gauges and ammeter. A separate dash facia sat at the extreme left and held the push button controls for the automatic gearbox (when fitted), and knobs for the headlamps and wipers. When fitted with a 4-speed manual gearbox, a floor mounted Hurst gear stick was used, while for automatic transmissions, a centre console mounted between the two bucket seats held the sporty ball-shaped shifter. Heating controls sat above the radio and ashtray in the centre of the dash.

By the spring of 1964, exterior bodywork was available in sixteen shades, including Black, White, Light Tan (Light Gray), Medium Tan Iridescent (Medium Gray Metallic), Light Turquoise, Medium Turquoise Iridescent, Dark Turquoise Iridescent, Ruby Red, Medium Red Iridescent, Light Blue, Medium Blue Iridescent, Dark Blue Iridescent, Copper Iridescent, Ivory, Gold Iridescent, and Barracuda Silver Iridescent. The last three were unique to the Barracuda and not available on Valiants, but no

Dodge Challenger & Plymouth Barracuda

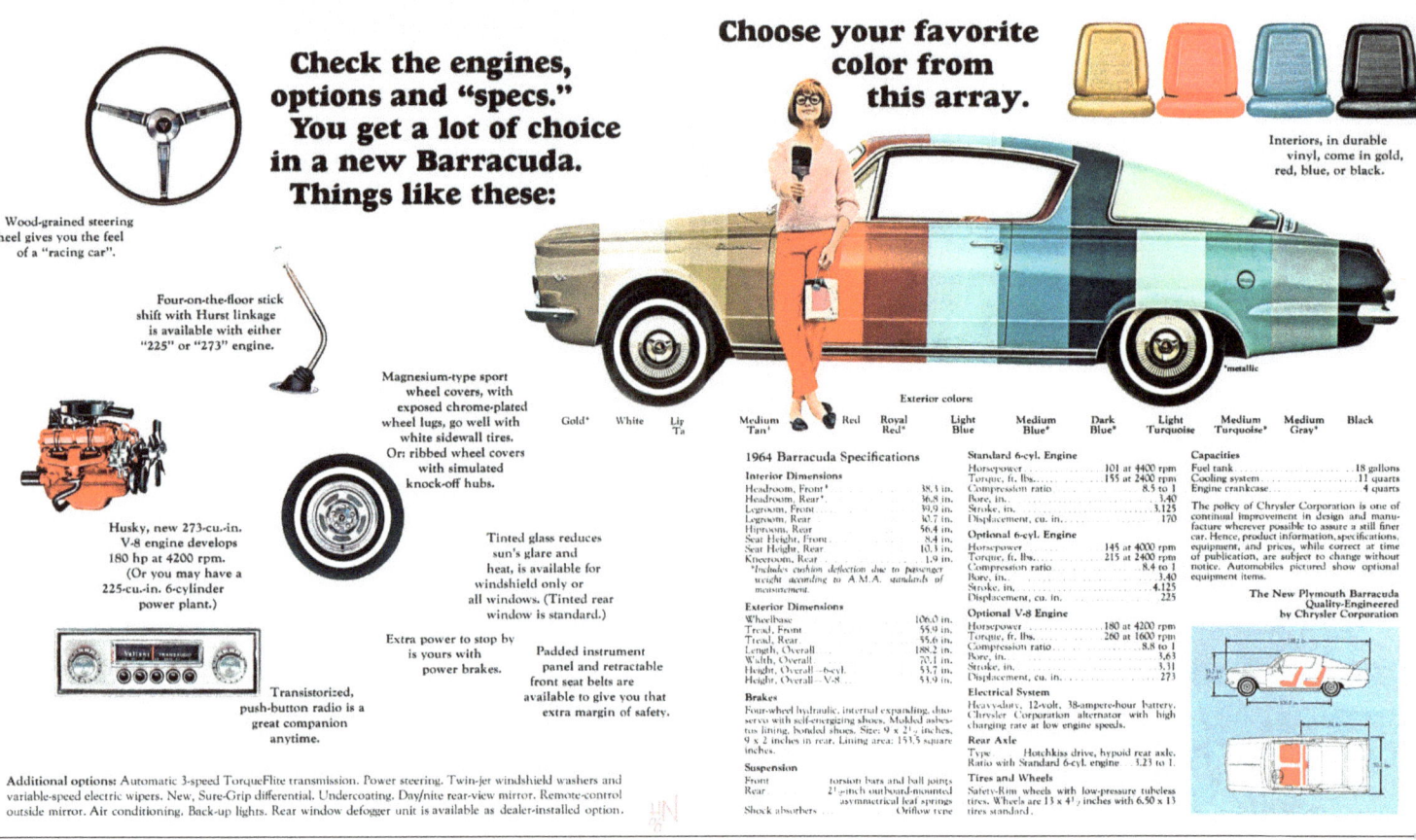

Still with the brochure, this shows the thirteen body color options and the four interior vinyl choices.

two-tone options were available as was the case with the other Valiant models.

Because the Barracuda shared its underpinnings and lower panels with the already successful Valiant, it was a very cost-effective and relatively simple car to create, overcoming possible problems caused by the uni-body construction technique. Design time and tooling were cut in half, and time means money! This was also how Chrysler managed to beat Ford to the dealerships by two weeks, no mean feat, and not achieved by accident. The car utilised Chrysler Corporation's signature torsion-bar front suspension and a solid rear axle on leaf springs at the rear. Like other Valiant coupes and sedans, the Barracuda rode on a 106.5in wheelbase and stretched out to 188.2 inches long overall.

Other than the roof and badges, the only other significant alteration differentiating the Barracuda from other Valiants was a chrome bar that emanated from the main headlamps, splitting the front grille into two halves, and holding large European-styled round parking lights at the other end of the bar, close to the centre. It retailed for a competitive price of $2365 (the Mustang sold for $2320). The trouble with it being so obviously a Valiant fastback was that Valiant did not have a youthful image at all; more for the frugal, sensible Americans that were looking for economical, family transportation. It also wasn't available in convertible form. This was reflected in the results

Taken from the base 100 series Valiant, the front grille also carried parking lamps close to the central meshed section, neatly splitting the outer portions and giving the car a European sports car look. (Courtesy Chrysler Historical Dept)

1964 Barracuda rear. The rear of the car held the largest single piece of glass ever seen on an American production car. Made by the Pittsburgh Plate Glass Company, it measured 14.4ft^2 and was made by using the 'sag method' instead of pressed glass. Many cracked when in production at PPG or on the Valiant assembly line in St Louis. (Courtesy Chrysler Historical Dept)

Dodge Challenger & Plymouth Barracuda

This publicity shot shows a car registered through Raynal Brothers, a Chrysler dealership situated at 9103 Chalmers Ave, Detroit, Michigan.

This was one of the few adverts aimed at a youth market. When first introduced, Plymouth did not emphasise the Barracuda's sporty nature and generally targeted the young family or economy minded.

from the relatively short sales season that ran from April to October 1964. The Barracuda managed a respectable 23,443 units, but compared to the Ford Mustang, which was introduced on April 17, 1964, and saw 126,538 units sold in the same time frame, sales were disappointing. It is worth remembering though, that the Barracuda did not steal sales away from other Plymouth or Chrysler vehicles – these were all new buyers – whereas the Ford Mustang took from the Falcon's catch.

Looking at what defines a pony car, power was never the main requirement. First and foremost it had to have an affordable base price, wear attractive sporty styling, handle well, and offer an extensive options list, including 6-cylinder and V8 engines. The last requirement was use of aggressive, youth-oriented marketing and advertising. The Barracuda offered all of this except for perhaps the latter point. The brochures for the first Barracudas in 1964 stated that it was a car "for people of all ages and interests," whereas Ford's Mustang and Chevrolet's Corvair were marketed almost purely at young professionals and the youth market.

Standard power for the Barracuda came from Chrysler's famously indestructible slant six overhead valve engine. In this case the slant six displaced 225 cubic inches, breathing through a Carter one-barrel carburettor, and was rated at 145 horsepower. The standard transmission was a 3-speed manual with a 3-speed automatic as an option. The only optional engine in the Barracuda was a mild 273 cubic inch version of Chrysler's small-block family of overhead valve V8s that sucked in air through a two-barrel Carter carburettor and was rated at 180hp. It made the Barracuda marginally faster, but hardly anything to get excited about. The Barracuda may not have set the automotive world on fire but it did receive some great reviews. *Road and Track* magazine had already described the donor Valiant as "one of the best all-round domestic cars," so the Barracuda was expected to be a well-balanced car from its inception.

This image shows a pre-production car for 1965, but it is actually a 1964 Barracuda, borne out by the Valiant badge on the front fenders. The sports stripe was introduced as an option late in 1964 and was continued in 1965 with the Formula S. (Courtesy Chrysler Historical Dept)

"Plymouth's new Barracuda is surely a winner if public interest is any indication," wrote *Motor Trend* in 1964. "Everywhere we stopped our Barracuda test car, people bombarded us with questions. It got so bad that we finally started parking at the deserted ends of streets and lots just so we could slip away before a crowd gathered. A more positive indication of the car's future lies in the fact that the Barracuda's production quota has been increased three times since this model's introduction." According to the magazine's first test, the Barracuda took 11 seconds to reach 60mph and completed the quarter mile in 18.2 seconds at 79mph. So the Barracuda was far from a muscle car, but where it did excel was in its handling characteristics, being able to out-maneuvre any of its competitors, as a true pony car should.

Even before the first Barracuda had been released, John Samsen and the others in the Plymouth studio and engineering were working on the 1965 version and a performance and trim option called the 'Formula S' package. The 1965 Barracuda

The 1965 Barracuda went virtually unchanged except for the loss of the Valiant name on the rear and large V on the front fenders. This year did see the introduction of the wonderful Formula S package, though. This included heavy-duty front torsion bars, heavy-duty rear springs, firm ride shock absorbers, sway bar, tachometer, optional rally stripes, extra wide wheel covers, special Goodyear Blue Streak 5.50 x 14 wide oval performance tires on wide-rim 14-inch wheels, unique 'Formula S' medallion, and a new V8. (Courtesy Chrysler Historical Dept)

VALIANT BEGINNINGS

Gail Bowers' lovely 1965 Barracuda sports the round Formula S medallion of the front fender. The wheels are correct for the period though aftermarket additions. With 64,596 units sold, this was the best year ever for sales of the Barracuda, but stole many of these sales not from the Ford Mustang, but its luxury sister, the Valiant Signet. (Courtesy Marc Rozman)

This shot clearly shows the heavy chrome trim that covers the trunk hinges, and the chrome bar inside the cavernous trunk that restricts forward movement of luggage when the back seats are folded flat. (Courtesy Marc Rozman)

Beautifully restored interior of this 1965 Barracuda shows a simple yet elegant dash, revised from the previous year. The instrument cluster now has two large pods holding the speedo on the left and the fuel, amps, and oil pressure on the right. Note the matching rev counter to the left of the instrument cluster. This Formula S has a 4-speed manual gearbox with floor mounted shifter. (Courtesy Marc Rozman)

At the heart of the new Formula S was a new 4-barrel, 235hp version of the Commando 273 V8. A hot high-lift, high-overlap camshaft, solid lifters, lightweight domed aluminium pistons, dual-contact breaker points, unsilenced air cleaner, and a Carter 4-barrel AFB carburettor all helped to increase brake horsepower. The 3-speed manual transmission was the standard pairing with the 273; a 4-speed manual or 3-speed TorqueFlite automatic was on the options list. This beautifully restored example is owned by Mr Gail Bowers. (Courtesy Marc Rozman)

Dodge Challenger & Plymouth Barracuda

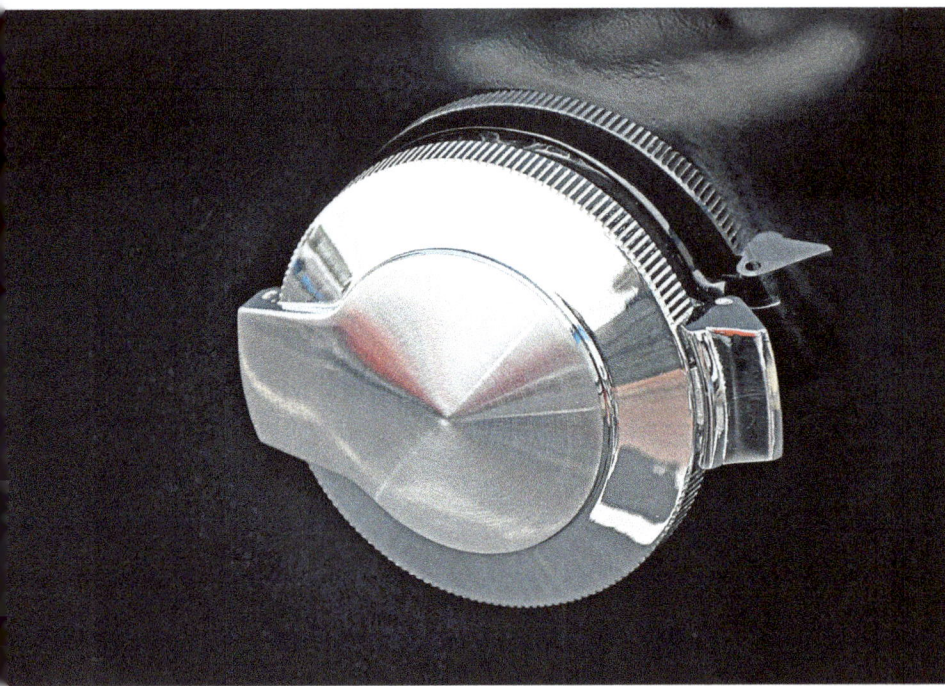

Attention to detail was important for the stylists at Chrysler. Even the fuel filler cap was of a sporty design. (Courtesy Marc Rozman)

went virtually unchanged except for the Valiant name badge disappearing from the right-hand corner of the deck lid and the introduction of the aggressive looking fish emblem, leaving the main changes to the Formula S package. The superb Formula S included heavy-duty front torsion bars, heavy-duty rear springs, firm ride shock absorbers, a sway bar, tachometer, rally stripes (optional at $31), extra wide wheel covers, special Goodyear Blue Streak 5.50 x 14 wide oval performance tires on wide-rim 14-inch wheels (replacing the usual 13-inch wheels), a unique 'Formula S' medallion designed by Dave Cummins and a new 4-barrel, 235hp version of the Commando 273 V8. A hot high-lift, high overlap camshaft, solid lifters, lightweight domed aluminium pistons, dual-contact breaker points, unsilenced air cleaner, and a Carter 4-barrel AFB carburettor all helped to increase the brake horsepower.

The 3-speed manual transmission was the standard pairing with the 273; a 4-speed manual or 3-speed TorqueFlite automatic was on the options list, along with disc brakes that could be fitted by dealerships. With a top-end speed of 110mph and 0-60 in just 8.5 seconds, this car was no slouch, but with its tough suspension to help it through the corners, it was almost perfect.

Modified front end styling gave the Barracuda a more European look, but it still resembled the Valiant too closely. Note the unique Formula S ornamentation on the fender. (Courtesy Marc Rozman)

1965 Brochure. In Canada, it was still being called the Valiant Barracuda in 1965, and offered buyers the optional "273in^3 V8 with power-pak that will make you think you're jet-propelled." Barracuda designer John Samsen said, "I owned a 1965 Barracuda Formula S, and liked it very much. Once, on a newly finished stretch of I-95, I put the 'pedal to the metal' to see how fast it would go, and the speedo needle passed the 125 mark and pointed straight down." Interior vinyl colors were now blue, red, black or gold.

Front-end style matches fastback flair: image is sporty!

Dodge Challenger & Plymouth Barracuda

(Right and below right) 1965 Concept. In 1965 the designers in the Plymouth studio were working on facelifts and had a light work schedule. Over September and October of that month John Samsen found the time to come up with a new design for a Barracuda. It featured concave hood, deck and rear window. Plymouth studio manager Gerry Thorley liked the design so Samsen did a number of sketches of it. Gerry got the authority to do a full-size clay study. The design was well liked but deemed too different from the cars of the day; Chrysler could not afford another show car at that time, so the idea was scrapped. (Courtesy Brett Snyder)

This option sold for just $3169, compared to the cost of $2535 for a standard V8-powered Barracuda. Inside the car was a revised dash that now used just two large pods, with the left still holding the speedometer and the right containing the temperature, fuel and ammeter. New on the options list was a 6000rpm tachometer that when ordered sat just to the left of and below the steering column, making it hard to read. Interior colors were Blue, Red, Black or Gold, all made in vinyl.

"Fitted with Barracuda's top engine option," wrote *Motor Trend* in its January 1965 test of a Formula S, "our test car had Chrysler's excellent 4-speed transmission topped off with a Hurst shifter. A 3.55 axle plus a limited-slip differential made our Barracuda able to leap from rest to 60mph in 8 seconds flat and sail through the quarter-mile traps in

Valiant beginnings

Even before the first production cars had started rolling off the Valiant assembly line, Plymouth designers were working on the next few years of facelifts. This sketch, drawn by John Samsen in 1964, shows the sports stripes and front grille for the 1966 Formula S package. (Courtesy Brett Snyder)

a shade over 16 seconds. Its biggest problem was wheel spin. Keeping it at a minimum took some doing, because the willing V8 would climb right to 6000 rpm and more in what seemed like no time at all."

The Formula S not only performed well on the street, but also won the 1965 SCCA rally championship. Due mostly to this popular option, sales increased dramatically to 64,596 for 1965, but still paled into insignificance compared to the 559,451 Mustangs sold by Ford, which was also now available as a fastback along with the convertible and hardtop. Ford also surprised the Chrysler guys with the introduction of the 289in^3 V8 in the Mustang. This gave up to 271bhp in the high-performance range. Brochures for both years' Barracuda were almost identical,

DODGE CHALLENGER & PLYMOUTH BARRACUDA

Although of poor quality, these important images show the first finished full-size clay models of the 1966 Barracuda fastback. Note the truncated rear screen, offering a more traditional rear deck, and unusual rear light arrangement that did not get as far as the production models. (Courtesy Milt Antonick)

The revised grille shown in Samsen's sketch is a reality but the racing stripes, optional with the Formula S package, have not been used in this publicity shot from Plymouth division. (Courtesy Chrysler Historical Dept)

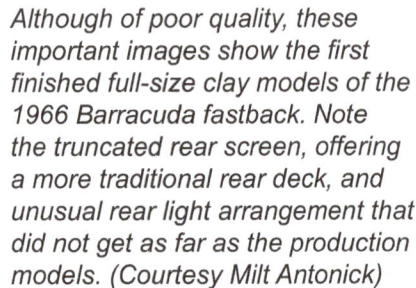

with just the Valiant badge on the trunk lid being airbrushed out of all rear three-quarter view images. If you couldn't stretch to the Formula S package, there was the alternative Rallye Pack, which included all of the heavier-duty suspension items: increased number of semi-elliptical rear leaf springs leaves, stronger torsion bars and shock absorbers and a 0.82in diameter front sway bar. This pack, along with the 273in³ V8 with the 4 barrel carb setup, and power brakes cost just an extra $156. All Barracudas came with Chrysler's 5 year, 50,000 mile power-train warranty. Regardless, the Barracuda was finding its feet and gaining popularity.

When the following year's Barracudas arrived in dealership showrooms on November 25th 1965, they had received a modified grid-pattern grille, new taillamps and more substantial bumper externally. A revised dash for the interior saw the demise of the corporation's much loved push-button gear changer in deference to a more traditional column-mounted shifter for the 3-speed auto. A longer centre console sat between the redesigned bucket seats and held the 'T'-bar changer for automatic shifting of the 4-speed

VALIANT BEGINNINGS

This is Milt Antonick's first drawing of the Barracuda before he stylised it to become an ornament for the production cars. (Courtesy Milt Antonick)

transmission. The all-vinyl interior now came in five colors: P4X Black, P4B Blue, P4Y Citron, P4H Red and P4V Tan/White. Barracuda scripts were added to the front fender in front of the wheel well, and thin pin-striping ran the whole length of the car. Stainless steel moldings covering the wheel openings also came as standard. A vinyl roof covering appeared on the options list and was a popular choice with buyers. Cars fitted with the Formula S package also had a round 'S' medallion below the Barracuda script. Except for the introduction of a disc-brake option, there were no big changes to performance. The Barracuda did have some success on the race track.

In 1966, the Sports Car Club of America (SCCA) created a new class called the Trans-American Sedan Championship. This Trans-Am series offered the opportunity for head-to-head competition between Dodge Darts, Plymouth Barracudas, Ford Mustangs and Chevy Corvairs. The rules were simple: competition was allowed between 'Production Touring Cars' with a maximum wheelbase of 116in. The competition was divided into two classes – an 'Under 2 litre' class (predominantly small European sedans) and the 'Over 2 litre' class (displacement limited to 5.0 litres, or 305in^3). The Trans-Am class rules stipulated that very few modifications could

Dodge Challenger & Plymouth Barracuda

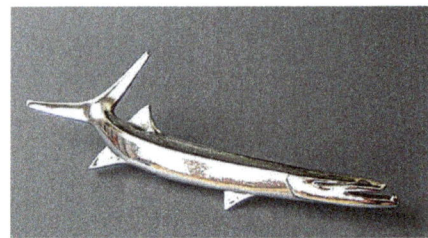

The Barracuda emblem was a stylised fish that adorned the cars from 1966 onwards. Designed by Milton (Milt) J Antonick just after fellow designer John (Dick) Samsen named the new car Barracuda, instead of the planned Panda nametag.

be carried out on a production car, but drivers were allowed to remove bumpers, rear seats, and floor mats. Exhaust mufflers could be replaced with straight-through pipes, and different wheel rims could be used so long as the stock rim diameter and width were maintained. Some famous names took control of Plymouth's sporty car, including Richard Petty, Bob Johnson, Bruce Jennings and Charlie Rainville. In the second race of the season, Bob Johnson took the chequered flag at the Mid-America meeting in St Louis in his Barracuda, while other teams consistently finished in the top 5 places with Barracudas or Dodge Darts. These factory-backed teams found marginal success in its start-up year, but Chrysler executives decided that the Trans-Am competition didn't attract large enough crowds to justify continued support, so Chrysler withdrew after only one season.

The frantic fish

If Chrysler wasn't impressed by the sales figures prompted by Barracuda's Trans-Am results, it must have been pacified a little by the results seen at the drag strip. Many drag racers used the early Barracudas almost from inception, and by 1966 they were a common and very successful sight at the drag strip.

One of the more unusual uses was by a new group of racers called 'wheel-standers.' The first unintentional wheelie car was the Maverick's Little Red Wagon that started doing wheelies when a Hemi engine was placed in the bed of the little Dodge pick-up in late 1964. The driver, Jim Golden, found he could still control the diminutive truck, even with two wheels dangling in the air. Such was

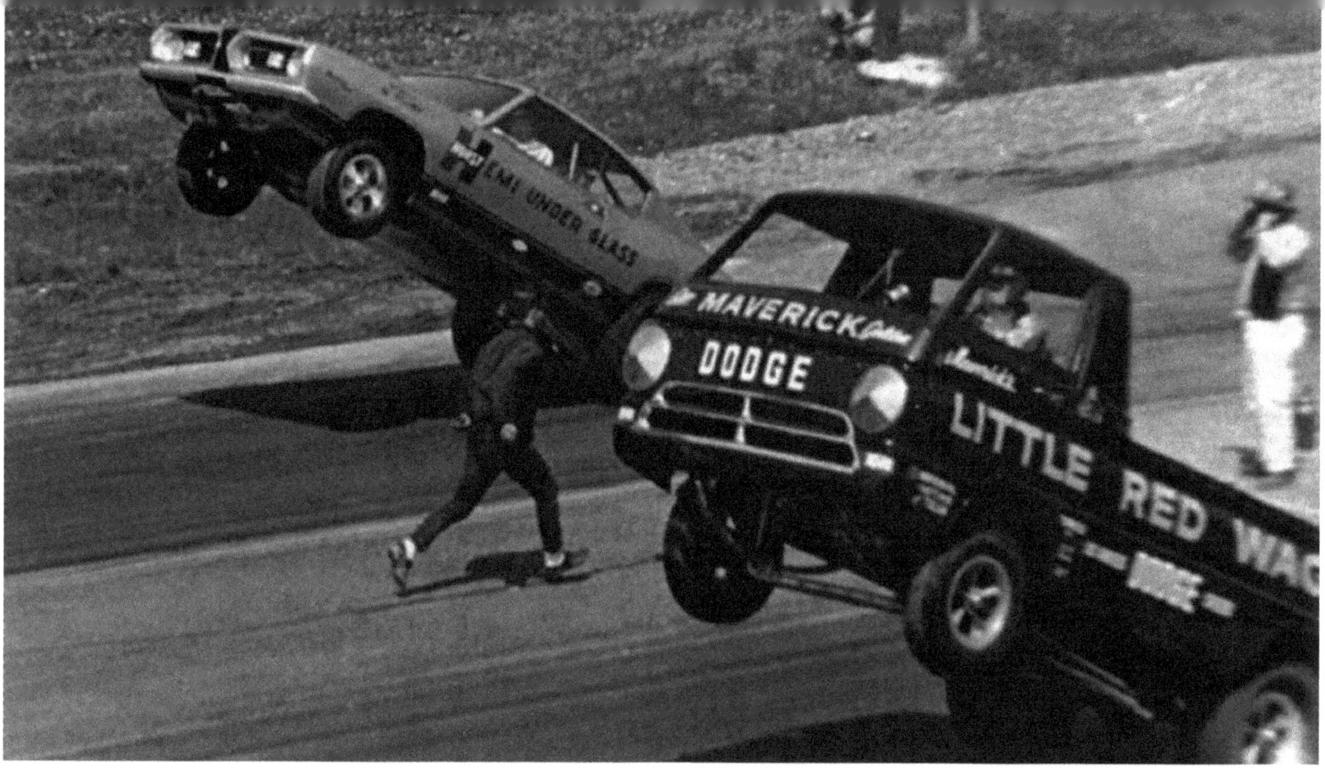

Here Hemi Under Glass takes on the very first wheelstander, Little Red Wagon at Gary, Indiana. The Dodge A-100, was also powered by a 426 Hemi, fitted with a Hilborn fuel injector unit. The engine was bolted behind the cab, in front of the rear wheels, which required cutting a hole in the pickup bed and another in the cab itself. The truck was built by Dick Branstner and Jay Howell in Chrysler's Woodward Avenue garage in Detroit, and was driven by Bill 'Maverick' Golden.

This advert for Hurst Performance Products appeared in the April 1965 edition of Hot Rod *magazine. George referred to George Hurst, the owner of the company. He was known to occasionally run shotgun in some of the Hemi Under Glass exhibition runs.*

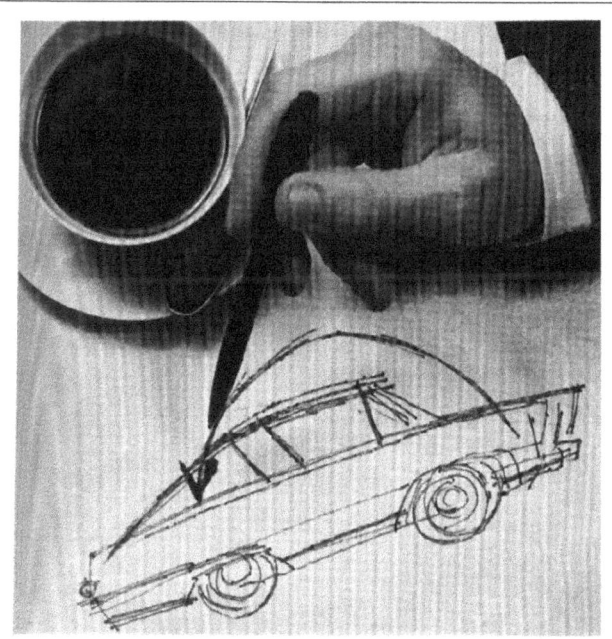

"We'll drop a Hemi in the rear," George said, "and run like hell."

That's the way the whole thing started, over coffee, George and the Hurst Performance Research designers kicking around ideas. You see, the primary purpose of the Hurst Research Center in Detroit is the development of ideas related to performance and safety. First, we go to the source to dig out the problems, asking the opinions of drivers and experts in the field. Garlits, for example, talks about chassis design and the problem of getting max horsepower to the strip. On the other hand, with super stock, FX and gasser speeds climbing all the time, Ray Brock suggests that safety and handling should be prime concerns of the experimental designer. While the Detroit original equipment engineers tell us they watch the drag strips to see what new ideas can be adapted for production automobiles.

The question that day at coffee: what type new vehicle should we experiment with? The conclusion was, a street machine that could be reworked extensively and turned into a rolling research lab.

There it was. George saw it and scratched it on the tablecloth and now it's a reality.

A Barracuda with a 426 Hemi where the rear seat used to be. A Barracuda like none you've ever seen before—with Hurst-designed chassis, suspension and driveline components: such as an inverted transmission, radiator in the trunk, independent rear suspension, and naturally a 4-speed stick and George's new custom wheels. (Write for details about his shifters and wheels.)

The Barracuda now goes by the name of "Hemi under glass"—a black and gold bomb that will appear at main events across the country. Look for it—another Hurst contribution to safety and performance through research. Hurst Performance Products, Glenside, Pennsylvania 19038.

HURST

One of the most memorable drag cars was the Hurst Hemi Under Glass. Originally piloted in 1965 by a super stock driver called 'Wild Bill' Shrewsberry, this Barracuda wheelstander was a major attraction at drag meets across America. After its first season, Hurst mechanic Robert 'Bob' Riggle became the regular driver, updating the same drivetrain each year until the car retired at the end of the 1971 season. It was replaced by a 1972 Challenger Funny Car. Riggle retired from drag racing after flipping yet another Hemi Under Glass, this one built around a Dodge Charger, in 1974.

In 1992 Bob Riggle came out of retirement and started to recreate his former ride. With the support of Hurst Industries and fellow enthusiasts, Bob built an awesome 1966 Barracuda complete with supercharged engine. In 1995, Riggle completed another version of his amazing car, the one you see here, built on a 1968 Barracuda.

The monstrous Hemi V8 runs on alcohol and creates 1500bhp. Not only does it do wheelies at a constant 30 degrees, it can run a quarter mile in under 12 seconds.

Valiant beginnings

the response from the amazed race-goers that he stopped racing and started booking himself in for exhibition runs. Very shortly after, drag racers started placing large engines into their cars where the back seat should be, and linked them to the differential via a complicated transfer box. On acceleration the front of the cars would pop up in a wheelie. Arguably one of the most famous wheel-standers was Bob Riggle and his Hurst Hemi Under Glass. The first Hemi Under Glass was built in 1965 using a new Barracuda and a 426in^3 Hemi V8. Built by Hurst Industries, Inc, it used an 8.75in Chrysler banjo-type transfer unit that was mounted backwards and upside down, so the pinion housing faced rearward. Its first pilot was a super stock driver called 'Wild Bill' Shrewsberry, who managed to get all four wheels to leave the ground at its first meeting, when the Barracuda reared up onto its back bumper. Shrewsberry left after the '65 season so the mechanic on the project, Bob Riggle, took his place. The car was dismantled and recreated to look like a 1966 Barracuda.

The next few seasons saw the car develop, along with Riggle's expertise in steering it. By 1969 the car was new again, and steerable. Riggle set up a steering brake beside the 4-speed, floor mounted shifter. Linked to the open-type diff, it used separate callipers on each wheel. He pulled the Hurst pistol grip once to go right and pushed it once to go left. There was a separate set of callipers to stop the car completely. He also modified the surplus firewall and floorpan with a large hole, so that he could see where he was going. The wheel-standers started racing each other for ETs and to see who could pull the longest wheelie. This last incarnation of the Hemi Under Glass lasted until 1975, when Riggle moved back home to Arizona. In 1992, Bob Riggle revived the Hemi Under Glass project with a 1966 Barracuda, and by 1995 had completed a replica of the 1968 model, too. He continues to amaze crowds around the world with his extended, full-track wheel-stands.

A Barracuda also appeared on the big screen, although in modified form. Legendary car customiser George Barris heavily modified a 1966 Barracuda for the teen flick *Fireball 500* starring Frankie Avalon and Fabian. The film involved moonshine runners getting involved in a road race and fighting for the affections of a girl. The musical film has many good race scenes using hot rods and production cars of the time. The car, named after the film, had its roof removed and a two-seat race car cockpit fitted along with a 426in^3 Hemi. The wheel wells have been radiused with a larger opening to compensate for the 700/12.50-13 Firestone tires. These tires were mounted on Rader spoked racing wheels made of aluminium with a chrome steel rim. The Hemi received an Isky drag racing cam used in combination with Jahns high domed racing pistons, and a 4-speed Ansen posi-shift gearbox was installed with the combination of 3.55 rear end gears and 13in wheels. Dual 4-barrel Ram-thrust manifolds and Holley carburettors helped with the breathing, while dual Dupree chrome dome electric fuel pumps were used to keep a steady flow of gas. Eight Ram-thrust inlet air tubes extended from openings in the hood for direct air into the carburetion system on the engine. Even with the extra bodywork and strengthening it was still relatively light, and was rumoured to be capable of 160mph in a quarter mile drag. To complete the transformation, forty coats of hand rubbed lacquer called Fireheat were applied. This consisted of multicolored blends of white pearl of essence faded into gold Murano, blended throughout in reflective gold leaf, carried through into Kandy Tangerine, then blended into translucent Kandy Red and finished off in burgundy. It took four men and six days of spraying to blend these multi colors from white into soothing burgundy. The paint was topped off with flames down the sides. The Fireball 500 was later made into a plastic model kit by AMT/Ertl.

For the 1966 model year, Dodge division was finally offered the fastback Barracuda body for its Valiant-based Dart, but declined the offer, instead giving a fastback design to the new and larger Dodge Charger. As for the Barracuda, another 38,029 examples were built this model year, which ended production of the first generation. The motoring press generally regarded the little Plymouth as a stable and adequate car, with acceptable handling and satisfactory power, but it just didn't have that X-factor, the sexy pizzaz that came with the reskinning of the Falcon to create the Mustang. The guys at Chrysler hadn't given up yet though, and with the pony car war just starting to warm up with Chevrolet, Pontiac and Mercury all preparing to enter the fray, the Barracuda entered 1967 looking all new.

Mr Riggle and his car were the star attractions at Lord March's prestigious Festival Of Speed in England in 2001. So great was the attraction that the unprecedented decision was made to ask him to come back, which he did in 2003 and again in 2007, with Riggle now in his seventies, still at the wheel.

Fireball 500 was a George Barris creation for the film of the same name. It was based on a 1966 Barracuda fitted with a 426 Hemi.

2
SECOND GENERATION 1967-1969

The second Barracuda continued to be built on the A-body platform shared with the Valiant, but now it wasn't just a Valiant with a fastback roof, but a whole line of cars in its own right, with its own sheet metal, and it did some catching up with the Mustang. As the Barracuda became more curvaceous, its donor car became more square – there could be no confusion between the two anymore. Once again, the Barracuda was introduced almost two months later than other Plymouths, on November 25th 1966, and for 1967 the Barracuda fastback (body code BH29) returned with all-new styling and a smaller rear glassed area that covered far less acreage. The Sport Barracuda, as the fastback was now called, had a backlight that arched gently across the rear end and blended into metalwork instead of curving right down to the rear wings, then stopped abruptly at what Plymouth optimistically called 'an aerodynamic spoiler.' There was also a new notchback coupe (BH23) with a rather odd-looking swooping roofline all its own, and a pretty new convertible (BH27). The three Barracuda bodies directly paralleled what Ford had been offering since 1965 in the Mustang line. Dodge, however, continued to make do with performance versions of its boxy Dart, such as the GT, and its more muscular and larger fastback Charger, but the difference between pony car and muscle car was now getting smaller and smaller.

Work on the second generation cars was started in 1964. This is a concept from John Samsen, showing how he wanted the next Barracuda to look. Although the 1967 cars didn't end up as sleek as this, the Coke bottle sides of the 1970 E-bodies can be clearly seen here. (Courtesy John Samsen)

Work on the new design started in late 1964, with most of the Plymouth studio working on ideas supervised by Plymouth chief stylist Dick McAdams. Recently appointed John Herlitz had just been hired directly into the Plymouth studio from college at the Pratt Institute in July of that year, but had spent a semester working at General Motors for experience, so it is no surprise that his designs had a fresh look about them that was inspired by cars produced by GM at that time. These smooth lines caught the attention of executives visiting the Plymouth studio, and it was Herlitz's overall design that was initially picked for the new '67 cars. His design was created

The Barracuda S-X show car is little known today. It was designed by John Herlitz in the Plymouth studio, shortly after joining the company. He had spent some time at General Motors when it was working on its Pontiac GTO and was inspired by the design. When the Barracuda S-X was shown to the public, GM quickly objected, and Chrysler Corp took the show car off the circuit before many people had seen or photographed it. John Samsen says, "Despite this problem, the Plymouth division execs wanted the 1967 Barracuda to use the S-X styling theme. As Herlitz left for National Guard duty, Milt Antonik and I were given the responsibility of directing the design work on the new body which still used the Valiant platform. I worked out the front end and hood, Antonik and Dave Cummins developed the fastback body and rear end. It was a team effort, and probably several other Plymouth designers contributed to it.

as a full-size clay model, and then a rolling shell built in fibreglass, which became the Barracuda S-X show car that was displayed in 1967.

When the S-X was shown to the public, GM objected vigorously, saying it looked too much like its new Pontiac GTO, so Chrysler Corp took the unusual step of removing the show car from the circuit before many people had seen and photographed it. Despite this problem, the Plymouth division bosses still wanted the 1967 Barracuda to use the S-X styling theme.

In an interview for *Forward* magazine, Herlitz explained the thinking behind the new car. "There were three approaches to the program, from an investment/budget standpoint. The first approach was to do another Barracuda like the first generation, which was essentially an evolved Valiant. The second approach was a complete reskin of the Valiant to make the Barracuda a completely separate car line. The third approach was to do an all-new car. That was the one I got to work on and that was fun! We took it to the point that the company was considering

Leading from S-X styling, other designers in the Plymouth studio had their take on what the 1967 line should look like. This is by Fred Schimmel and dated September 1964. (Courtesy Brett Snyder)

Another John Samsen sketch for the 1967 series, this one dated 25 August 1964, showing the similarity in bodysides with accentuated ramping over the wheelarches. Samsen's sketch shows gills on both front and rear fenders. (Courtesy Brett Snyder)

This is Milt Antonick's initial proposal for the second generation Barracuda. A full-size clay placed in front of a Mustang for comparison purposes. Hints of styling for the third generation can be seen here, although little was taken from this clay for the second generation. Milt explains the thinking behind this design. "Nick O'Shea and Roy Tobias did the clay for me in just four days. As with a number of new proposals it went back to the clay machine only to be utilised later. For the G (1967-69 A-body) Barracuda program I moved the rear fender form aft, softened the side horizontal break line, utilised the roof shape, added a Kamm-style rear form and kept the floating bumpers. Note also it has no flush C-pillar. Concave wheel-lips were added to improve the fender to wheel relationship caused by the Coke bottle body form. This detail was taken from my 1955 Fisher Body Craftsmans Guild model car." (Courtesy Milt Antonick)

These Polaroid snaps show the clay model for the 1967 notchback designed by John Samsen. He was also responsible for the front grille and hood styling seen on all of the production Barracudas for that year, while colleagues Milt Antonik and Dave Cummins developed the rear end and some of the side detail on the full-size clay model. (Courtesy Milt Antonick)

buying Jaguar of England and getting them to build the car. Unfortunately, they couldn't make the deal work financially, so they took the theme we came up with for the all-new car and had Dave Cummins retrofit that theme to the second approach, the reskin of the existing Valiant." This went on to become the fastback version. Unfortunately for Herlitz, he was temporarily called away for duty with the National Guard, so the clay model stage was handed over to John (Dick) Samsen to develop.

"It was decided to have a smaller backlight than that on the previous Barracuda," Samsen told me recently. "I designed the 'notchback' model for 1967 and revised the front end and hood, while Milt Antonik and Dave Cummins developed the fastback body and rear end on the full-size clay model. We needed a new grille for the car that would allow

Second generation 1967-1969

Another shot of the notchback clay just after completion in the Plymouth studio. It is representative of how cramped the studios were at Chrysler in the 1960s and early '70s. Note the early hood from that was revised before production. (Courtesy Milt Antonick)

a lot of air to pass for the more powerful V8 engines which needed a bigger radiator. I had always liked 'real' eggcrate grilles, but high cost kept them out of most car designs. I was sitting in the studio looking up at the ceiling when I noticed the aluminium egg crate light diffusers fitted on the strip lights. I managed to get hold of a spare diffuser and cut it down to fit the new opening. It looked good and the production department said it was robust enough to do the job so we used it." The new grille also held the squared-off side lights. The fastback was designed first, with the convertible and notchback thereafter, with all three sharing the same lower body panels and brightwork. Dave Cummins' talent kept the side panels smooth and uncluttered, while matching front and rear bumpers were given a European look by Milt Antonick, 'floating' separately from the car.

Milt takes up the story of the body development of the 1967 Barracuda: "I wanted that body to be offset from the roof form at the C-pillar and have a gentle undulating form reflected in plan view (a

This was the team that created the 1967 Barracuda. From left to right: Dave Cummins, William Shannon, John Samson, Richard McAdams, John Herlitz (seated in the car), Jerald Thorley, Irving Ritchie and Milt Antonick.

Publicity shot of the production Barracuda fastback for 1967 featuring a much smaller glassed area, but the trunk was still huge and kept its fold down rear seat arrangement. The engine bay had been enlarged to accept the big 383in³ V8 but left little room for ancillaries. Note the sports pop-up filler cap on the rear flank. (Courtesy Chrysler Historical Dept)

Coke bottle). The Avanti shape had about twice as much form as the Barracuda both in side view as well as plan view. The form, as a result, moved too far outboard from the wheels, so the wheels looked lost. As a result we moved the entire body form inboard including the sill, which was possible due to body on frame construction. Hawk seats would not fit and a hurry-up narrow fibreglass Alfa copy was utilised. With the Barracuda, because of uni-body construction, the sill position was retained. I think the rear wheelhouse inner was retained as well along with the side glass position. To solve the wheel to sheet metal relationship I used a concave wheel lip like the shape on my Fisher Body model. There is an offset character line low on the front fender taken directly from the S-X, which I think was John Samsen's idea. The Kamm rear form was inspired by a German book on aerodynamics given to me by designer Bob Doehler."

Antonick was also responsible for the chrome 'snap-open' racing gas cap. In an interview he gave me recently, Antonick explained: "The Triumph TR3s

Second generation 1967-1969

Plymouth did some catching up with the Mustang when it introduced a convertible and notchback version of its slippery fish. The unusual roofline of the notchback hardtop coupe still proved popular, selling just over 28,000 units in its first year. (Courtesy Chrysler Historical Dept)

and TR4s had the external snap-open gas cap, and it just seems like the right thing to do on a sports car. I bought one of the Indy-type caps, a big, aluminium thing about 5in in diameter off the shelf from an auto parts supplier that specialised in British sports cars on Woodward Avenue. When you snapped it, it made a hollow popping noise. I took it back to the studio and started popping it as Design Chief Elwood Engle walked by. He saw it and said, 'Let's put that on the car.' Which is exactly what I was hoping he would say!" The cap was mounted high up on the left flank of the car to minimise intrusion of the filler pipe inside the car. This would be copied by Dodge for its Charger a year later.

The convertible came with a power top and glass rear window as standard, while the notchback coupe and fastback were available with a vinyl roof from the options list. The interior changed again, with bench seating and the centre armrest being the standard fitting on the hardtop models, while bucket seats were standard on the convertible and optional for the other body styles, along with a matching centre console. The front seats flipped forward a long way which, along with the wide-opening doors, made entry and egress for rear passengers relatively easy. The famous fold-down rear seat on the fastback version remained, including the huge carpeted cargo area. The fastback also had the advantage of having pillarless driving because the rear quarter-lights disappeared into the body when wound down, leaving a panoramic side view for all occupants. The convertible and coupe had a more traditional trunk space with the spare tire being fitted in a well, hidden by a false floor. A revised dash saw two large instrument pods sitting either side of a half-size central pod which held a vacuum operated 'performance indicator' that could be swapped for a tachometer.

The left pod housed the speedometer which, as standard, showed 120mph or optionally, a 150mph dial could be fitted. In the same housing was the trip odometer. The right-hand pod held the alternator, gas, temperature and oil pressure gauges. The whole panel was finished in neat brushed aluminium. Headlamp switches were placed on the far left along with the hazard warning lights, while the washer/wiper switch sat to the right. The heater was fitted in the same position above the centrally-mounted radio.

All Barracuda body styles were available with the Formula S performance package and included Red-Line tires and hood ducts. The best of the catch was the beautifully simple convertible. With its clean lines, devoid of over-ornamentation, the soft-top Barracuda looked sleek and slippery, helped because the power top sat so low in the down position under a tonneau cover, the smooth, straight lines going unimpeded.

Dodge Challenger & Plymouth Barracuda

Plymouth was "out to win you over" with the new notchback Barracuda.

One of the prettiest convertibles of the 1960s was the Barracuda. Minimal extraneous trim and smooth, simple lines make this a classic car that still looks good today.

With its new sheet metal, all models were longer (by 5in) and wider than the first incarnation, but not much lower, and it would not be unfair to say that this design arrived at the wrong time. Although Virgil Exner and Chrysler had championed the long hood/short deck dimensions with the Valiant and 1962 Plymouth range, which was then picked up by Ford and GM, the new Barracuda

SECOND GENERATION 1967-1969

1967 Barracuda convertible.

for 1967 moved away from this, sticking with a more traditional long hood/long deck proportion. Ironically, the introduction in 1967 of the Chevrolet Camaro, Pontiac Firebird and the Mercury Cougar, all with long hoods, short decks and low bodies, made the new Barracuda look instantly dated. When Plymouth did finally adopt the accepted sporty car dimensions on its 1970 Barracuda, its profile looked almost identical to that of the 1967 Camaro, while ironically, the new 1970 Camaro

Unlike many of its competitors, the Barracuda convertible was still a handsome car whether the top was up or down.

Another publicity shot of the '67 fastback, this one clearly showing the big heart on the front bumper. The heart with the little tail was at the centre of Plymouth's 'out to win you over' campaign that kicked off this year.

wore a fastback roof that seemed to be a direct copy from the 1967 Barracuda.

The 1967 Barracudas did have some fans though. *Car & Driver* magazine, although describing the first Barracudas as aesthetic disasters, said of the 1967 Barracuda, "it has tautness of line and an integrity of design matched by few American cars of any vintage ... unquestionably, the best-looking car out of Detroit in 1967," while the British magazine *Autocar* stated "The Barracuda has the advantage over its two main competitors (Mustang and Camaro) in being available from the factory with right-hand-drive. Not just for this reason, but because of its ultra-smooth transmission, punchy engine and better than average adhesion, our staff were unanimous in liking it more than the others of its kind."

Because the new Barracuda was still running on an A-body, albeit with an extended wheel base from 106in to 108in, the suspension continued to be torsion bars at the front with leaf springs at the rear, identical to Valiants and Dodge Darts. Extra leaves were fitted if the car came with the largest engine or heavy-duty suspension option. A choice of four engines were available, with the 225in^3 slant six or

SECOND GENERATION 1967-1969

1967 Sports (fastback) Barracuda Formula S with E70 x 14in road wheels designed by John (Dick) Samsen booted with Goodyear Red Streak wide oval tires as part of the S package.

The competition was hot in 1967. The Mustang received its first moderate restyle this year with a new front end and tail, but the overall shape went unchanged until 1969. This is a 1967 Mustang fastback.

Hey fellas, do you think we could squeeze a big 383 into that little Barracuda engine bay? Yeah? Okay, well let's do it! The new Commando 383in³ V8 became an optional extra available on the fastback Barracuda S version, and left no room for power steering or other ancillaries.

the 2-barrel 180bhp 273in³ V8 being the standard offerings, with a 235bhp version of the same V8 fitted with a 4-barrel carb, and a new Commando 383in³ V8 as optional at extra cost, although the 383 was only available on the fastback Barracuda S version.

Even though the engine bay was larger than the Valiant-based car's by a good 2in, it was still a tight fit for the new 383 so it had to wear a modified and restricted exhaust manifold, limiting the motor's power to 280bhp. For the same reason, it also meant that power steering and air conditioning

Dodge Challenger & Plymouth Barracuda

Along with the revamped Mustang, the introduction in 1967 of the Chevrolet Camaro, Pontiac Firebird and the Mercury Cougar, all with long hoods, short decks and low bodies, made the new Barracuda look instantly dated. This is a Mercury Cougar from 1968.

were not available with this engine either (although a redesigned power-steering pump would find its way under the hood later in the year). Offering 400lb-ft of torque at 2400rpm, this was still an engine with a lot of punch, and with chromed valve-covers and a crackle-painted air cleaner, it looked pretty impressive too. Braking was provided by drum brakes all round, although front disc brakes were optional on all V8s and standard with the 383. Because the 383 engine added another 300lb to the weight of the car, buyers and reviewers at the time seemed to prefer the 235in^3 V8 with a 4-barrel carb setup as the best balance between performance, weight and control.

Advertising for the '67 Barracuda was now aimed entirely at the youth market, with the division as a whole telling buyers "Plymouth is out to win you over," seen with a red heart and curved arrow symbol. The advertising in national magazines also focused heavily on the cars outstanding manoeuvrability, with headlines like "You'll never want to go straight again," complemented by images of a fast cornering car. Its performance marketing worked so well, only eight percent of buyers opted for the slant six engine. Sales rose dramatically from the previous year's low of 38,029 to 62,534 units, of which 30,110 were fastbacks, 28,196 coupes, and 4228 convertibles. Many Plymouth followers and industry

Second generation 1967-1969

These two photos dated 25 October 1966 are grille texture studies for the 1968 Barracuda. Milt Antonick explains, "The grille outlines were modified near the center of the vehicle. The purpose was to increase the opening and gain more cooling. We were considering going to an all-plastic grille, and first attempts restricted air flow compared to the metal egg crate texture. The 'heat-sink' final design worked well and did not require a grille opening modification."

experts thought it deserved better sales, but, up against increasing competition from newcomers Mercury, Pontiac and Chevrolet, it is understandable why they weren't higher.

1968 The beat goes on

"This fish purrs, growls, and produces long low whistles. The new Barracuda from Plymouth." That's what the adverts claimed for 1968, but cosmetically, there was very little change except for the introduction of some safety and emissions equipment dictated by the government. The most noticeable difference to the interior was a change in knobs and dials, while a Rallye package allowed for a wood-grain style appliqué on the dash, which complemented the wood-style door panels and simulated wooden 3-spoke sports steering wheel.

On the outside it was a matter of refinement, with subtle changes to the hood ornament and front grille. The hood ornament remained quite plain on the base models but denoted engine displacement when fitted with the 340 or 383 'S' package. The grille now featured fluted vertical strips while the Plymouth nameplate moved off-centre to the left. All cars received round side marker lights as standard, while at the rear of the car the taillights underwent a mild redesign that encompassed the reversing lights within the taillight setup.

The growling mentioned in the advert was caused by a new power plant under the hood. Chrysler introduced its new small-block 340 V8 across

Second generation 1967-1969

The rear of the car saw a mild redesign of the taillights that encompassed the reversing lights within the taillight setup. This British registered fastback also had standard road wheels with chrome 'dog dish' centre caps.

the corporation and Plymouth used it for its Barracuda Formula S package. The Formula S was still the best value for money, with a host of items from the options list built in as standard, including the 4-speed manual transmission fitted with a heavy-duty clutch (or an automatic transmission as an alternative), heavy-duty suspension, wider wheels booted with red or white stripe wide oval tires, dual exhausts, sill moldings and a full complement of instrumentation. All of this mated to a powerful 340in³ V8 engine.

The 145bhp 225in³ slant six was still the standard engine for base Barracudas, while the 273 V8 was dropped completely, making the 318 the base V8 engine attached to a 3-speed manual gearbox. The fresh 340 had a huge effect on the Barracuda. Not only was it a supremely good engine, its more diminutive size allowed for easier access for servicing and ancillaries like air conditioning and power steering to fit with ease under the hood. But this engine really cooked! Weighing in at only 539lb, the 340 could produce 15 per cent more power than the redundant but larger 273in³ V8 fitted with a 4-barrel carb.

Although the main block was related to the LA engine family, the 340 had thinner wall castings, making it much lighter, but engineers at Chrysler had also created a new design for the head that featured larger intake and exhaust ports. They stated

The Plymouth heartbeat still went on, but the heart was pumping a bit faster for 1968. The beginning of the ad read "So you're coming up to the Christmas tree and the exhaust is going bappetybappetybappetybappety and all those little internal bits are going whumpawhumpawhumpawhump and you're out to grind the sound barrier into bite-sized equations with your howlin' Barracuda."

that the new engine achieved 275bhp, although it was proved by independent establishments to be nearer the 290 mark. The heavy 383 was still available, with an increase in horsepower up to 300bhp made possible by a redesign of the manifolds and head, but most buyers preferred

DODGE CHALLENGER & PLYMOUTH BARRACUDA

Plymouth was already using the term 'Cuda in its advertising, a year before it introduced an official 'Cuda model. This Sports Fastback was the main image from the 1968 Plymouth brochure and is wearing many extras from the options list, including body accent stripes (available in five colors), bumper guards, wire wheel covers designed by John Samsen, red streak oval tires and a white vinyl roof.

"Barracuda likes to go places. To beach parties. Deb parties. Church socials. Blasts. Wedding receptions. And the corner grocery." They pretty much had it covered for 1968, but the youth market that had been buying pony cars for the last few years was growing up and settling down to have a family. The market was beginning to change already.

the small block. The balance between power and weight was superb. In 1968, *Motor Trend* magazine tested the heavier 383-powered Barracuda mated to an automatic transmission, summing up with: "The 383 engine eliminates air conditioning and, more importantly, power steering – and

SECOND GENERATION 1967-1969

Big news for 1968 was the introduction of the superb 340in³ V8 engine. Weighing in at only 539lb, the 340 could produce 15 per cent more power than the redundant but larger 273in³ V8 fitted with a 4-barrel carb. Although the main block was related to the other LA engines, and shared the same 3.31in stroke, the bore was 4.04in and featured thinner wall castings (making it much lighter), a drop-forged crank, more substantial rods and aluminium alloy pistons with notched flat-tops. But engineers at Chrysler had also created a new design for the head that featured larger intake and exhaust ports. They understated that the new engine achieved 275bhp at 5000rpm and 340lb-ft of torque at 3200rpm, although it was proved by independent establishments to be nearer the 290bhp mark.

One of the all-time great American sports cars was the Barracuda S fitted with the 340in³ V8. Almost a forgotten part of automotive history, it had a phenomenal mix of raw power and agile control on the road. This restored 'matching numbers' example is part of the VerHage collection in Holland, MI. When originally sold in Pennsylvania it had a sticker price of $3683.90. (Courtesy Marc Rozman)

that additional 106 pounds of engine weight up front and 242 more pounds of car without mechanical assistance make it a two-fisted stormer meant for the slab-shouldered he-man who wants to know what's going on down there."

It still managed to hit 60mph in 7.8 seconds, and the quarter mile in 15.5 seconds at 92mph. Other journalists of the time managed to get 0-60 times of under six seconds when using the 340. Oddly, with all this power available, the optional front disc brakes were only purchased by 6.1 per cent of buyers when they weren't fitted as standard. The advertising also changed tack in 1968 with new cartoon style advertising for all Plymouths. Aimed purely at the youth market, the colorful posters demanded attention and helped the Barracuda gain more respect as a street and strip performance car. Plymouth produced a total of 45,412 Barracudas during the 1968 model year, with the fastback remaining the most popular with 22,575 units sold – 19,997 hardtop coupes, and 2840 of the handsome convertibles.

The simple but elegant hood of the 1967 to 1969 Barracuda was designed by John Samsen. With the introduction of the 340 V8 in the Formula S package, the call-outs were placed on the side of the hood bulge. (Courtesy Marc Rozman)

Second generation 1967-1969

Hemi Barracuda Super Stock

Since its inception, drag racers had been stripping out the lightweight Valiant and Barracuda and dropping big-block engines into the engine bay. Factory-backed racers were dominating the strip, and with its increasing interest in performance, it was only a matter of time before Chrysler engineers at the Woodward Avenue garage tried to shoehorn the mighty Hemi engine into an A-body car – and this they did successfully in 1968.

The Barracuda S/S was a racing-only version of the fastback street car powered by a 426 drag Hemi. Chrysler engineer and member of the Ramchargers Dick Maxwell was the main force behind the venture. In an interview many years ago, he explained how the funding for the most radical Chrysler to date was found. "We usually had to get sales division approval to do something like this. The race group at that time was in product planning. The first thing we could do was go to the product planners and sign them up in supporting the program. Then we'd go to our leader, Bob Rodger, and get him behind it, then the sales divisions and sell them on it, which wasn't hard because there was so much enthusiasm for racing in those days and drag racing in particular because of the muscle car boom. Once we had that done, it was a matter of scraping up money, which was sales division money, to pay for the program."

Maxwell wanted to see the engine in a Barracuda and Dodge's similarly engineered Dart. Because they shared the same drivetrains and dimensions, it was decided to build just one prototype, or 'mule' car, a Plymouth Barracuda. They tested everything on the

The Barracuda Super Stock was a racing-only version of the fastback street car, powered by a 426 Race Hemi. The front of the car had to be modified extensively, including the relocation of the front suspension shock towers, moving the battery to the trunk, moving the brake master cylinder, the production of an air scoop for the hood, and fibreglass panels, including the hood and fenders. Weight was the enemy, so the interior was stripped almost bare, along with removal of the heater, body sealer, sound deadening material, exterior mirrors and even the right side seatbelt. It came with lightened Dodge A-100 van seats, lexan glass, straps for window mechanisms and little else inside. Even the steel doors and bumpers were made of lighter steel, taking overall weight down to approximately 3000lb. Each car had a window sticker stating it was not to be used on public highways, only for use on 'supervised acceleration trials.'
This is a photo of the Plymouth 'Mule' car built in 1967 to test components for the following year's Hemi-powered SS cars. Mule cars were built for a single purpose: to be driven to the point of structural failure, to see how much abuse they could take. (Courtesy Chrysler Historical Dept)

This is just a small part of the VerHage collection. VerHage has been selling cars since 1914 when Henry VerHage set up in Hudsonville, MI. Lloyd, one of Henry's five sons, began the Holland location in 1963 selling Chryslers. Over that time the business has collected an enviable assortment of Mopar classics. With no fewer than six Barracudas in the collection, the Verhages are big fans of the car. In the foreground is a 1968 Formula S followed by a 1969 Formula S convertible, then a 1969 'Cuda 440 and in the background, a 1969 Formula S with a 383, a 1968 Barracuda fastback, and a 1964 Barracuda. The collection is opened to the public once a year, on the last Saturday of September. (Courtesy Marc Rozman)

mule in 1967, writing a manual for the car as they went. On completion of the trials, production was turned over to Hurst Industries, which set up a production line in Hazel Park on the outskirts of Detroit. Chrysler delivered stock Barracudas and Darts to the facility, where they underwent modification. The front of the car had to be altered extensively, including relocating the front suspension shock towers, moving the battery to the

Dodge Challenger & Plymouth Barracuda

The 426 drag Hemi was first introduced in 1964 and was used in Chrysler's factory-built drag cars through to 1968. Over those years the engine got lighter, mainly through the increased use of aluminium and magnesium components, including heads, oil pump body, oil pump cover, water pump housing and alternator bracket. The NASCAR Hemis used a different intake manifold to the one seen here.

Milt Antonick worked on this fibreglass one off hood scoop for the Barracuda Super Stock. It was passed over for another intake that sat higher up from the hood to make the most of airflow over the body. (Courtesy Milt Antonick)

trunk, moving the brake master cylinder, producing an air scoop for the hood, and creating fibreglass panels including the hood and fenders.

The exact number of Super Stockers built depends on whom you talk to, but it was at least fifty and possibly as many as seventy-five. Maxwell was quoted as saying: "We had no trouble selling those cars. We originally scheduled fifty of each, and we had so many orders we went back and built twenty-five more. We built seventy-five of each." They could be ordered through ordinary Plymouth and Dodge dealerships using the standard Barracuda/Dart order form and selecting body code B029. The cars were delivered in grey primer so that teams could add their own paintwork and decals, and could be had with either a 4-speed manual gearbox (code 393) or the Torqueflite automatic (code 395). It is thought that 61 were fitted with Torqueflite automatics and the rest with the manual box. Hurst supplied special headers, custom shifter linkages for the manual box and modified heavy-duty Dana rear-axle assemblies.

Weight was the enemy, so the interior was stripped almost bare along with the removal of the heater, body sealer, sound deadening material, exterior mirrors and even the right side seatbelt. They came with lightened Dodge A-100 Van seats, lexan glass, straps for window mechanisms and little else inside. Even the steel doors and bumpers were treated, taking the overall weight down to approximately 3000lb. The cars were immediately successful, with one of the first recipients, Ronnie Sox, managing times of mid-10 over the quarter mile with the Sox & Martin Barracuda with very little modification, and by 1969 he had won the Super Stock class at the Spring Nationals.

Each car came with a window sticker stating it was not to be used on public highways, only for use on 'supervised acceleration trials,' and came with no warranty whatsoever. Every buyer had to sign a disclaimer stating he understood that there was no warranty and the car did not conform to Motor Vehicle Safety Standards; having said that, many of these cars survive today and are frequently driven on the public highway. Many are still raced, and remain almost unbeatable in their class. Although the Street Hemi had been introduced on larger Plymouths in 1966, the public would have to wait a while longer before the Hemi could be found under the hood of normal production Barracudas.

ONE OF ONE

If you were looking for something really unusual, then how about a car that was one of a kind? Although Barracudas were a popular export, and were converted to right-hand-drive configuration on arrival in a country, this particular 1968 Barracuda (below) is unique. It is believed to be the only right-hand-drive Barracuda built at Dodge Main Plant, Hamtramack for the US market, and was built in October 1968. It was specially ordered by Admiral Thomas Crudders, Royal Navy, while he was on a posting from England to Washington. He bought and ordered the Forest Green notchback from LP Steuart, Inc, a long-time Chrysler Plymouth dealer at 14th and P Streets, Washington.

Ticking the options boxes #680 for RHD and #021 for a 225in^3 slant six, the car was also ordered with power-assisted front disc brakes, Torqueflite transmission, heavy-duty suspension including front anti-sway bar, the 325 light group, radio, black vinyl bench seats with white door panels and trim, front heater with defroster, rear demister, bumper guards front and rear, and a right-hand exterior chrome mirror to match the standard left-hand item.

After its delivery, Crudders used it on the streets of the capital for almost a year, but his choice of right-hand-drive was not made on a whim – his plan had always been to send it to England at the end of his posting abroad. The Admiral obviously had friends in very high places, because on his return to the UK in September 1969, Admiral Crudders had his car flown back by the RAF into RAF Lyneham, Wiltshire, on a new C-130 Hercules – an unusual way to transport personal belongings today, but almost unheard of then. From there it was tested and registered as PMR 40H. It was used regularly but not excessively every year until the Admiral died in Bishop's Waltham, Hampshire, in 2001. Heather Flahearty, the Admiral's daughter, then sold the car onto its second and current owner, Tony Oksien, also from Hampshire, in late 2001. The car was still complete and with no major rust, but quite tired and in need of some TLC. Tony pledged to the Admiral's family that he would restore the car to its original 1968 glory. In 2003 Tony started work on returning the car to its former prestige, and after four years of labour it was finally finished, and has been seen at quite a few Mopar car shows already, still with only 41,000 miles on the clock and ready to give valued service for another forty years.

It was sad and tired but still serviceable. This is how PMR 40H looked in 2001, just another Plain Jane Barracuda hardtop coupe. But this is one special car – the only right-hand-drive Barracuda built in Detroit for the American market. Specially ordered by a Royal Navy Admiral while on a posting to Washington, he brought the car back to England in 1969 and used it until his death in 2001.

Seen here in 2008, the car is back to its former glory, Forest Green paintwork glistening in the British summer sun. (Courtesy Tony Oksien)

It's second and current owner, Tony Oksien, spent four years carrying out an extensive restoration. The interior received a complete makeover including new white vinyl upholstery and carpeting.

The 225 engine looks like it has just been fitted on the Plymouth production line.

1969 THE 'CUDA SWIMS IN

The 1969 model year ran from 1 August 1968 until 31 July 1969, and except for a slight change in the grille pattern, block lettering in the rear aluminium valance, and a change in the side marker lights, there was little to distinguish the cars from the previous year's offerings. The most obvious way would be those side marker lights; the 1967 Barracuda had no side marker lights at all, the 1968 model had small circular ones, and the 1969 model had much larger rectangular markers.

Formula S cars were more refined, becoming one of the best sports cars available in the '60s. When fitted with the 340 V8, it became a true driver's car that caressed the road with its perfect balance of power and agility, a car for people that understood and appreciated sophisticated handling. It came with recalibrated suspension pieces along with larger E70 x 14 Red Streak tires, powerful disc brakes, and a Hurst shifter if you went for the 4-speed manual gearbox. They had their engine displacement badge positioned below the barracuda badge on the front fenders, while the round Formula S medallion moved to the taillamp panel.

Dodge Challenger & Plymouth Barracuda

The light weight of the Barracuda has always made it attractive to drag racers, and enthusiasm for these great cars has not dulled over the years. This shows a 1968 Barracuda ripping down the quarter mile at Santa Pod Raceway in England in 2008. Owned by Matt Bailey, it has a Ray Barton Hemi under the hood. (Courtesy Tony Oksien)

1968 Formula S. The options and package list was a long read in 1968, and included a Décor Group that offered luxury front bucket and rear bench seats, simulated wood-grain appliqués on door and quarter trim panels, a pedal dress-up kit and full carpeting. The Rallye Cluster Group included a simulated wood-grain appliqué across the instrument panel, a higher 150mph, calibrated speedometer, and a trip odometer. But the jewel in the crown was, of course, the Formula S, which came with most of the items within the other groups, along with a 340 or 383in^3 V8, heavy-duty clutch and 4-speed transmission, or high-speed governor and high-performance torque converter with the automatic transmission, heavy-duty suspension including anti-sway bar and firm ride shocks, heavy-duty wide rim wheels fitted with E70 x 14 Red or White Streak wide oval tires, low restriction dual exhaust system, bodyside sill molding, and Formula S ornamentation.

Hot Rod magazine managed to take a 340 Formula S through the quarter mile at 14.32 and 99.7mph, but even with unbiased and positive results like that, they didn't storm out of the dealerships. Sadly, only 85 convertibles, 325 hardtops and 1431 fastbacks came in Formula S 340 guise. Bold sport side stripes were introduced this year with the engine displacement stated within it on the front fender. The prize for craziest option must go to the Pop Prints or Mod Tops; a garish yellow floral vinyl roof covering and matching vinyl seats and trim aimed at the female buyer. Thankfully, it didn't prove to be too popular!

In late 1968, some 1969 model cars were fitted with a lightweight aluminium alloy road wheel (option W23), but they were found to be troublesome as the lug nuts would not stay tight. Extra torquing caused cracks in the wheels, so they were recalled, although a few sets escaped and are now worth a great deal to collectors.

Even the same engine line-up was on offer, but power was becoming increasingly important in the pony car war, with less emphasis on handling and a 'sporty image,' and Plymouth had a plan!

On the street and on the strip, the Barracuda had already picked up a cool abbreviation – 'Cuda – and in 1969 Plymouth released models that made the most of the slang term. Two low-cost, bare-bones 'Cudas went on sale available as either a fastback or coupe. The 'Cuda 340 and 'Cuda 383 offered heart-stopping acceleration and borrowed much from the Formula S package, but offered few creature comforts, while the S remained more refined and aimed at the connoisseur of driving rather than the all-out street racer.

Continued page 66

Second generation 1967-1969

The Barracuda was a great export commodity and enjoyed impressive sales in markets other than North America, selling in countries as far afield as South Africa, Australia, Switzerland and England. Most of these countries required that some of the car be produced within that market, even if it was only trim details. This is a right-hand-drive 1969 fastback Barracuda from South Africa, which differed little from the American model.

The car is badged as a Valiant Barracuda, as was the case for many years in overseas markets. It is in original and unrestored condition and has the 225in^3 slant six engine.

Badge and script from a 1969 South African Valiant Barracuda, positioned on front fenders.

One of the strangest packages available from any manufacturer was the Mod Top released on 9 September 1969. It consisted of a vinyl roof, matching vinyl seats and trim, all made in a lurid yellow flower pattern. If you didn't like the color, an aqua and blue pattern was available on the mid-sized Satellite. Not surprisingly, it didn't prove popular, though achieved enough sales to make it a worthwhile offering until the end of the 1970 season, by which time it had been enhanced by a floral decal for the rear quarter light window.

Dodge Challenger & Plymouth Barracuda

```
              FOR USE IN AUTO SHOW SECTIONS

MOD-TOP PLYMOUTH -- Colorful flower-patterned Mod-Top roofs
and matching interiors are offered for the first time on
the 1969 two-door hardtop models of the Plymouth Barracuda
and Satellite.  The Barracuda is a yellow and black pattern,
while the Satellite features a blue and green vinyl roof
and interior.

From:   Chrysler-Plymouth Public Relations
        P. O. Box 1658, Detroit, Mich.   48231      (68-4003)
```

Plymouth issued a press release about the Mod Top for distribution at motor shows. This image clearly shows the Mod Top logo on the rear quarter light. (Courtesy Barry Washington)

Seeing is believing! Tasteful it is not, but somebody bought it, and as this 2006 photograph shows, is willing to restore it. This Barracuda is in excellent shape, including the vinyl roof and seats. (Courtesy Barry Washington)

The pattern ventured as far as the door panels, as can be seen on this fabulous 1969 notchback. (Courtesy Barry Washington)

"See what Plymouth's up to now." That was its catchphrase for 1969, and by that year, the Formula S had become even more refined and is today classed as one of the all-time great American sports cars. Fitted with the sublime 340 engine, this was a match made in heaven. A powerful, lightweight mill paired with a well-built, well-engineered driver's car. This restored example lives in Holland, Michigan and has the larger and much heavier 383 mill. (Courtesy Marc Rozman)

Plymouth introduced the 'Cuda for 1969. A pared-down street racer that took the emphasis away from sporty driveability and onto gut-wrenching straight line acceleration. The 'Cuda was initially available as a 340 or 383, but in April 1969 Plymouth released the stump-pulling 'Cuda 440. Based on the B-block 383 mill, the 440 had a raised block to allow for a longer stroke. Being a big block it was a squeeze to get into the engine bay, leaving little space for other equipment like power steering or power brakes. With all that weight up front it may have been hard to steer round corners, but what the 440 could do was propel the occupants to 60mph in just 5.6 seconds. This was the biggest engine fitted to a street legal production pony car, and with their simulated hood scoops and matching twin black hood racing stripes, all of the 'Cudas were easily distinguishable. (Courtesy Marc Rozman)

Dodge Challenger & Plymouth Barracuda

The 'Cuda 340 and 383 used their respective displacement engines, of course, along with other performance parts like the Hurst shifter, heavy-duty suspension and tougher E70 x 14 tires. The 340 version used the same 275bhp rated engine offered in 1968, while the 'Cuda 383 was powered by the 330bhp version of the 383 engine found on the options list of its larger stable mates like the Satellite and Fury. The extra 30 horses were mainly due to a hotter camshaft. If that wasn't enough power, in April of 1969 Plymouth released a mid-year model 'Cuda 440.

Using the 2-door hardtop platform, Chrysler engineers shoehorned the big-block engine into the Barracuda's tight engine bay, but this left no space for what one might think of as almost essential equipment like power steering, power brakes or the disc brake option. Air conditioning? No way! So for drivers with large biceps that didn't like going around corners and had plenty of room to stop in, this was the perfect beast. With its 375bhp, the 'Cuda 440 could rocket from 0 to 60 in just 5.6 seconds, and cover the quarter mile within 14 seconds at 104mph. The latter was mainly due to poor traction – add some wide slicks to the rear and you could manage times in the low 12s and a terminal velocity of 110mph. This was staggering performance for a street-legal car.

The package was limited in what you were offered, too, with only the 3-speed auto-transmission or 4-speed manual gearbox, and a choice of two axle ratios: 3.55:1 or a 3.91:1, both fitted with a Sure Grip 8.75in Dana rear. Stronger torsion bars were fitted, but the same E70 x 14 tires were used, worn on 5.5in rims, as fitted to the less powerful engines. This was the largest engine available in any pony car of the time, and over-enthusiastic moving away would easily destroy the rear tires. The power was breathtaking and hard to handle. Excessive understeer was accentuated because of the stiffer suspension and the 600lb of engine weight riding so close to the front. With their simulated hood scoops and matching twin black hood racing stripes, all of the 'Cudas were easily distinguishable.

Aquatic Savage

Another easily distinguishable, but even rarer Barracuda was the Savage GT. This little known hybrid was built by the aftermarket performance parts company Auto Craft in the city of Fond Du Lac, Wisconsin, from 1968 through 1969, following the same path that Shelby was on at Ford, and Don Yenko was on with various Chevrolets.

An agreement was made that Plymouth would supply stock Barracuda S models of the same years to Auto Craft for heavy modification, adding a host of performance and safety features, then sell them through Plymouth dealers. The Savage was the vision of Auto Craft's young general manager and product designer, George Prentice Jnr. Prentice, along with a small group of friends from his high school days, set out to beat the Shelby GT350 Mustang at its own game.

Financial help was received from family members and Auto Craft, with the first prototype cars reportedly being made in Prentice's three car garage at home in West Bend, a town between Fond Du Lac and Milwaukee, WI. The cars, all fastback bodies, came with Crager SS-type chrome or Mopar wire wheels, lake pipes, vented disc brakes, a fibreglass trunk lid with a unique molded lip spoiler, a simplified flush-fitting grille that held rectangular turn signal/side lights, and a unique roll bar that wrapped snugly around the outside of the seats just at the level of the seat bottom, giving side impact protection. Suspended from the roll bar were racing harness seat belts that kept the driver and front passenger hugged tightly into the high-backed bucket seats. The matt black tail panel and front grille wore 'Savage' badges, and the fibreglass hood had an air scoop reminiscent of that fitted to the 1967 Hemi-powered Plymouth Belvedere.

Available with either a 340, 383, or a warmed 440 Magnum engine, it is thought that only thirteen Savages were originally built: eight with a 340 V8, four with a 383 and only one with a 440 Magnum. The 340 and 383 cars had engine dress-up kits, but were also fitted with bi-flow intake, tuned headers, dual point distributor, low restriction air filter, and a wilder cam. This pushed the 340 version up to 280bhp and the 383 V8 to 335bhp. However, the 440 had extensive work and pushed out much more than the advertised 380bhp.

The first production car was completed on April 24 1969, although both *Motor Trend* and *Car Life* magazine had tested a prototype in October of 1968. The writer at *Motor Trend* had perhaps been

Second generation 1967-1969

From 1967 through 1969 there was little change in the interior. Buckets seats were standard but the automatic shifter mounted in the console was optional. This 1969 'Cuda has woodgrain appliqués on the dash and console so was probably fitted with the Rallye package. The radio and extra gauges below the dash and on top of the steering column are aftermarket items.

The Savage GT hybrid was built by Auto Craft Company, Inc and had a host of performance and safety features that made it "The complete road car." Standard equipment included bucket seats, 8000rpm tachometer, solid wood steering wheel with Savage horn push, heater/defroster, 4-speed transmission, front and rear anti-sway bars including a Shur-Guide constant tension stabiliser, extra heavy-duty suspension and shock absorbers, electric fuel pump, special 14 x 6.0 aluminium wheels booted with 150mph-rated raised letter Dunlop radials, side exhaust pipes, full width brake lights, recessed instrument panel knobs, breakaway ashtray, and a unique anti-roll bar. The options list was even longer, and offered four-wheel vented disc brakes (something even Chrysler hadn't come up with yet), power steering, power brakes, air con, AM/FM radio or 8-track cassette player, tinted windows, real wood dash, electric clock, high-intensity driving lights, 180 degree panoramic interior mirror, three-speed Torqueflite transmission, centre console and adjustable head rests. (Courtesy Brad Barrie)

This is one of only four Savage GT survivors known to exist today. The front facia has been changed back to that of a normal production car, and although heavily modified for drag racing, as most of them were, it still carries some of the unique identifiers of these extraordinary cars. One of the eight originally fitted with a 340 V8 and 4-speed manual, it still has the unique interior roll-cage, seat belt overhead retractors, Savage steering wheel and medallion, Savage tail panel and side pipe cutouts under the car, as well as the original fender well header cutouts. It now runs a small block engine stroked to 415 cubes, putting out 625+hp. On the few occasions it has travelled the quarter mile, its owner, Brad Barrie, has achieved 11.11 seconds at 123mph. (Courtesy Brad Barrie)

Dodge Challenger & Plymouth Barracuda

Clearly visible in this interior view is the Savage real wood steering wheel and centre cap, and part of the unusual roll-cage that dominates the cockpit. It wraps around the side of the front seats for side impact protection. At the car's launch in Fond Du Lac in May 1969, Vernon R Hoppman, president of Route 1 and the Auto Craft Company, was quoted as saying, "The whole car is strictly performance and safety." Even the powerful engines had a safety aspect. "In an emergency, you can get out of somebody's way." He explained why Auto Craft chose the little Plymouth: "The Barracuda is more automobile than other comparable sports model cars in today's market, and because the Barracuda lent itself to what the designers wanted to do with it." (Courtesy Brad Barrie)

Parts from the Savage GT catalogue were available for purchase by owners of standard Barracudas. (Courtesy Brad Barrie)

sniffing too many exhaust fumes when he wrote his article, immediately after swallowing a dictionary. His anti politically-correct rambling ended on a positive note for the GT and he summed the car up as being "refreshing in a vulgar sort of way, or vulgar in a refreshing sort of way, depending on your adaptability." *Car Life* was more down to earth, but still adored the 383-powered car, only finding fault with the non-powered steering when it came to parking the little brute.

The Barracuda hybrid was aimed at the buyer who wanted a more unique model, something extra special, customised and more performance inspired. Although the Barracuda was already very European in looks and handling, by adding the GT moniker the car got a more European sounding name, too. With their Formula S handling, these Barracudas were the ultimate 'road' Mopar of the time.

Brochures and advertising were printed, offering the car for $4750 as either a fastback or convertible, but initial response was indifferent and no soft-tops

Second generation 1967-1969

This is Ronnie Sox, one of the greatest exponents in the art of drag racing, in the Sox & Martin 1969 'Cuda. This legendary team had a long and successful association with Plymouth.

These snapshots (below and overleaf, left) were taken in 1966 and show the fender vent or gill proposal for the 1969 Barracuda. The designers wanted to vent directly to the engine bay. The vent would have required retooling the fender, as well as modifying the inner panel. If they had indicated an area for a fender detail in the original fender die a provision could be made in the tooling for later use, as was done for the E-body later on, which allowed for the vents as an identity modification. The vents seen here were designed by Don Hood but were never used.

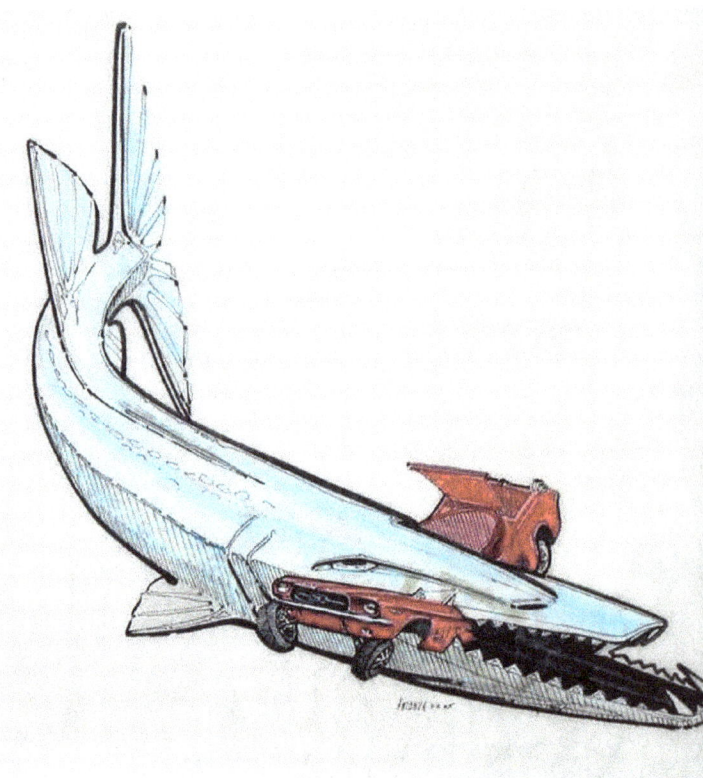

The competition between manufacturers was real, and Chrysler didn't like playing second fiddle to Ford's Mustang. Milt Antonick penned this light-hearted cartoon of a Barracuda munching on a Mustang for breakfast. It was done for the studio but it appeared in the Chrysler corporate newspaper. Antonick still has the original. (Courtesy Brett Snyder)

were ordered. The Auto Craft Company, Inc had invested quite a few dollars in producing parts for the cars, along with a small assembly line at a body shop in West Bend, so when they found out that Chrysler was to introduce an 'all-new' car for 1970, the cash-strapped little company threw in the towel. It is thought that only four are still in existence today, with only one keeping its original specifications.

Even with these performance-oriented models, sales dropped in 1969 with Plymouth building just 31,987 Barracudas – 17,788 fastbacks, 12,757 hardtops, and just 1442 convertibles. Today, the 1967-69 Barracuda models are all but forgotten, but were one of the prettiest, and in the case of the Formula S, most driveable sports cars ever produced in America. A Formula S fitted with a 340 V8 would be the one to look for; with a great balance between power, weight, and steering, it was a refined and superior sports car compared to many of its rivals.

No shrinking violet – 1970

The year 1970 was a pivotal time in American automotive history. As America saw a new decade dawn, motor manufacturers saw an ever increasing wave of resistance against sports and muscle cars. There were stricter federal regulations on safety and emissions like the 1970 Clean Air Act, a move by insurance companies to drastically increase premiums for powerful cars to the under 25s, and politically correct advocates of road safety like Ralph Nader bombarding Washington with accident statistics and demanding tighter controls. This would all eventually conspire to reduce the power of the pony and muscle cars. Into this miasma of woe was born what are arguably the ultimate, most sought after, and collectable pony cars ever built: the E-bodied Dodge Challenger and Plymouth Barracuda.

Work on an all-new Plymouth Barracuda started in February 1967, long before the storm clouds mentioned previously had started to gather, but Chrysler is a master at the art of mistiming cars. The emphasis on sporty cars had disappeared and the muscle car war was heightening in ferocity. Sales of the Barracuda, Valiant and Dodge Dart were being lost to the sportier-looking Camaro and Cougar, and lead times dictated that the earliest they could get a new car into full production would be the 1970 model year. Chrysler engineers were given the task of producing a new Barracuda with an engine bay big enough to fit any of the corporation's large array of engines – up to and including the mighty 440in^3 V8 – and just as importantly, have space left over for ancillaries like power brakes, power steering, and air conditioning.

There was no way that Chrysler was going to be left behind in the horsepower race. Dodge was already renowned for its performance cars and had a great range with the compact Dart GT, mid-size Coronet R/T and Charger, that were collectively known as the Scat Pack, but it too wanted something fresh to go up against the Mercury Cougar and Chevy Camaro. Dodge executives

This is one of the first sketches done for the 1970 Barracuda by Milt Antonick. These 10 minute quick draws enabled the stylists to play around with different concepts before committing to more time-consuming artwork. Antonick said "I did this one for my own benefit, and utilised it to develop the rear form because I did not like the designer proposals. I developed the rear of the '70 Barracuda from this as well." (Courtesy Brett Snyder)

Dodge Challenger & Plymouth Barracuda

Another one of the few surviving sketches of what Plymouth and Dodge stylists were aiming for in 1967 when they started work on the E-body program for 1970. This well-illustrated Barracuda concept is by John Samsen, and carries some styling cues that appeared on future production vehicles including the hidden wipers and rear taillamps. (Courtesy Brett Snyder)

made no secret of the fact that they wanted a part of the pony car market, so it was decided to build two almost identical cars on a new platform called the E-body: one for Plymouth and one for Dodge on a shortened B-body platform.

The general layout of the cars was done in Chrysler's advanced styling studio. This department had been created back in 1949, for and by legendary designer Virgil M Exner Snr. By 1967 this studio was under the capable watch of Clifford (Cliff) C Voss. It set all the parameters, including the wheelbases, how much greenhouse area to have, positions for side glass, and the angles of the windshield and doors sills, but even this wasn't as straightforward as

it could have been. Diran Yazejian, a retired Chrysler design executive, was working in the Dodge exterior studio when the 1970 Challenger was being styled. He claims that the 1970 E-body program was late because corporate management didn't quite know how to push the pony car program forward. When it finally decided to proceed, in order to make up time, the windshield, cowl, door hinging points, etc. were taken from the already underway 1971 B-body Charger/Satellite program and used as the basis for the new E-body.

Once the E-body had finally been created by the advanced styling studio, stylists in Dodge and Plymouth exterior studios competed in creating

Robert (Bob) Hubbach was another stylist working in the Dodge studio alongside the late Carl Cameron and Bill Brownlie. In 1962 Hubbach graduated from the Art Center School in Los Angles, CA and soon found employment in General Motors' Advanced Studio. In December 1967 he moved to Chrysler where he remained for the balance of his career. Hubbach was responsible for the hugely popular Australian Valiant Charger, and also planted the design seeds that grew into the modern Chrysler 300C, as well as having quite a lot to do with some of Chrysler's bolder statements, such as the Dodge Viper GTS Coupe and Roadster, the Chrysler Atlantic and Dodge Copperhead show cars. This is one of his ideas for the front end treatment of the new Challenger done in Prismacolor markers. (Courtesy Brett Snyder)

the outer skin to cover the basic E-bodies. Rivalry between the two styling studios was fierce, with no love lost. The mindset of the divisional personnel was as if they were two completely different companies, in bitter competition with each other. Under the direction of Elwood Engle, the body from the Plymouth studio was approved, much to the annoyance of the crew within the Dodge studio. From this rounded, sculptured design, Dodge stylists reluctantly had to form their unique sheet metal for the E-body, while the roof section (except for the window opening) and other exterior and interior panels were shared with Plymouth. Thus, the basic body looked the same on both cars.

Another idea from the same stylist, Bob Hubbach. (Courtesy Brett Snyder)

While engineers worked on the mechanics using as many available component parts as possible from the compact A-body and mid-size B-body – including axles, suspension and brake systems – designers in the Plymouth studio were given the basic shell and tasked with creating the outer skin. Chrysler bosses wanted something contemporary, so under the guidance of Plymouth studio manager Gerry Thorley and assistant Irv Ritchie, a team that included Milt Antonick, Dave Cummins, John Herlitz, Bill Shannon, Fred Schimmel, Pete Loda, Neil Walling, and John Samsen pooled their ideas to come up with the new 1970 pony car. Engle told the stylists that the sales division wanted a car with long hood/short rear deck proportions like the Mustang, but with a unique look. The Plymouth designers were very pleased to be able to move away from the slab-sided Ford-looking designs being offered on the larger corporation cars.

The late John Herlitz is generally thought of as the man responsible for the beautiful silhouette of the 1970 Barracuda. In an interview many years ago for *Musclecar Review*, he recalled "I wanted to pull the rear quarters as high as possible and spank the roof down as low as possible and just get the very high hunched look in the rear quarters, allowing the front fenders to become the long, leading design element that ran out past the power plant to give a very dynamic thrust."

This was following the theme he had started

No shrinking violet – 1970

Carl Cameron did both the back and front ends of the new Challenger, taking the grille he did for the stillborn 1967 Dodge Charger Turbine car. The company was seriously considering selling a turbine-engine Charger to the public as a follow-up to the 1963-64 Chrysler Turbine cars that the company loaned to families for a three-month evaluation. Carl designed a grille opening with a camera case bellows-effect leading the viewer back to a recessed grille. The grille had an egg crate texture that was derived from the similarly textured ceiling-mounted fresh air/heating ducts found in the studio. But most of the stylists in the Dodge studio had an idea of how the so-far unnamed new E-body should look. Here are some sketches from 1967, some more prophetic than others. (Courtesy Brett Snyder)

himself with the Barracuda S-X, but which had also seen the demise of the fastback. However, that famous 1970 bodyside resulted from a weekend activity that did not include Herlitz, but rather saw Elwood Engle, Roy Tobias, Nick O'Shea and the design manager of the project, Milt Antonick, working on drawings and the full-size clay model. Herlitz was actually responsible for less than 10 per cent of the surface design. This was reinforced very recently by Diran Yazejian. According to him, Elwood Engel went into the Plymouth exterior studio one Saturday morning to review the Barracuda clays. Engel was not happy with what he saw. Diran and a few clay modelers happened to be in the Plymouth studio that morning when Elwood noticed them. Motioning to clay modelers Nick O'Shea, Roy Tobias and Jack Avallito, Elwood asked them for help modifying one of the Barracuda clays. They worked the remainder of that Saturday and the next day as well. Elwood and Antonick came in that Sunday to personally direct the work. By Monday morning, the basic design of the '70 Barracuda was done.

They cleaned up the design utilizing a sketch by John Herlitz, but eliminated a pronounced character line in the front fender. Milt said "We utilised two clay models which allowed four variations. At that point the centerline profile was set, and small bodyside variations were being evaluated. Remember we received the package from the Voss Studio. This included a 58 degree windshield (we later managed to develop a 60 degree windshield for the B-body – the argument was night vision refraction of headlamps as a double image). The Voss package also defined the curvature and tumble-home of the side glass and the sill or rocker position, which is a structural member shared with the B-body. The rear glass was not defined, but we were told not to do a fastback. They wanted to tie the structure together in the C-pillar area. We added some front overhang and reduced the rear overhang as much as possible while still clearing the leaf spring hangers, similar to the Avanti approach.

"I think we spent about eight weeks developing the clay. I wanted to provide a gill or engine vent on the A-body Barracuda as a visual update, but could

Across the hall in the Plymouth studio, work was progressing with the clays for the Barracuda. Although the basic E-body shape can be seen in this snapshot taken by Milt Antonick in 1967, the front end shows a much clearer evolution from the 1967 to 1969 A-body Barracudas. (Courtesy Milt Antonick)

not because it would require re-tooling the fender from scratch. The stamping people said we could define an area for a fender update in the original fender design, and that is how we managed to add the fender vents (non-functional) later on the '71 models. They were designed by Don Hood."

Elwood Engle spent a lot of time going between the Plymouth and Dodge studios, guiding the two teams to a similar conclusion. The Plymouth designers were trying to overcome the problem of flaring out the hood form, and it was Engle who suggested they look at the engine cowling from the British Supermarine S6B floatplane that won the famous Schneider trophy from 1931 for inspiration.

This aeroplane featured protrusions on each side of the nose to aid streamlining when fitting the large Rolls-Royce Type R engine. The world-beating aircraft was designed by Reginald J Mitchell at the Supermarine Works in Hazel Road, Southampton, England, and was the forerunner of the Supermarine Spitfire. When later Spitfires began being fitted with larger, supercharged versions of the Rolls-Royce Merlin and Griffin engines, the same aerodynamic bumps first seen on the S5 and S6 aircraft reappeared, allowing clearance between the engine and body. Herlitz was responsible for refining the basic design concept done by Engel, along with detailing the front end, while the rear was done by Milt Antonik.

One thing that bothered Herlitz was the sharpness of the body's horizontal, front-to-back 'B'

Although not of great quality, this studio snap shows the silhouette to be used on the new cars, along with two more options behind it. It also demonstrates how cramped conditions were in the studios. (Courtesy Milt Antonick)

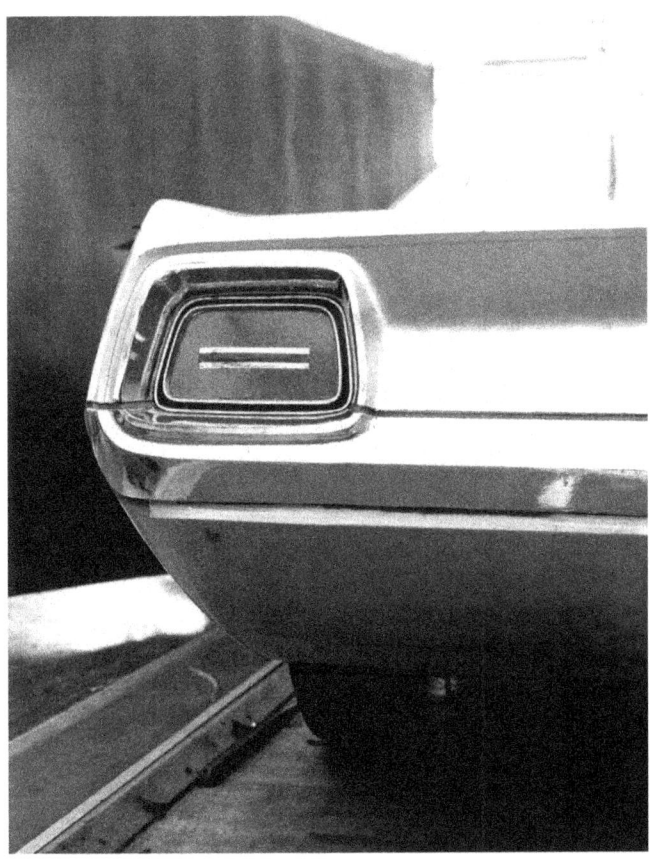

A 1967 photo of an early E-body clay taillamp possibly styled by Frank Backhouse. This design had the fuel filler behind a round filler door, but the idea was dropped because of the similarity with the Ford Mustang. (Courtesy Milt Antonick)

This is the first incarnation from the Dodge studio realised as a full-size clay. It is simply badged 'NAME.' Looking more like a Mercury, it would undergo dramatic changes before it would become a Challenger, although it does have the long hood, short deck and raked back windscreen. (Courtesy Brett Snyder)

line. Herlitz wanted the line to be rounded off, and Pete Sawchuk, who ran Chrysler Styling's drafting operations, promised him that it would be corrected on the body drafts. But it never was, much to Herlitz's annoyance.

As for the Challenger, Dodge Studio manager Bill Brownlie worked with designers Carl Cameron and Bob Gale on several concepts that looked more like the Mercury Cougar before they decided on the final, raised rear-deck design suggested by Engle and Herlitz, giving the car that classic 'Coke bottle' shape. For the most part, the new Dodge E-body was badged as 'NAME' throughout its development, although names such as Eliminator, Conquest and Explorer were tried. In an article in *Style Auto* dated 1969, Brownlie said "We wanted a space-age capsule for driver and passengers when we first explored the basic concept of the Challenger, and we accomplished it."

Brownlie came in one day to work on the full-size clay model, mapping out the rear quarter hop-up in the bodyside B-line. He then suggested carving away the clay above the B-line so as to add the scallop section present on the final design. Carl Cameron then did both the back end (with a car-wide taillight similar to his 1966 Dodge Charger), and the front end, reprising the grille he did for the stillborn 1967 Dodge Charger Turbine car. Turbine cars had their own cooling requirements, so designer Cameron developed a unique grille opening that was set

Milt Antonick was the stylist in charge of the development of the new E-body Barracuda. He took this photo of the hood scoop and fender vent clay studies in 1967. "I considered releasing the original Barracuda with fender vents but could not come up with anything fresh-looking, so decided to utilise the feature later with the hope of designing something worthwhile." (Courtesy Milt Antonick)

This photo shows a paper exhaust proposal for the 1970 Barracuda. Antonick explained. "We utilised paper overlays for grille, taillamp, and other details before committing the time and effort to clay modelling. At the time Chrysler was utilising leaf spring rear suspensions which prohibited the E-Jag or 'duck butt' undercut form below the rear bumper. I borrowed the Avanti approach of covering the rear spring shackle with a vertical nerf-bar form which allowed the surface to be modelled forward of the springs. Had we modelled the shape to the springs the result would have been a baggy pants look instead of the cool undercut look. Since the sheet metal was a separate piece we managed to get the exhaust to run through the part. This did not come easily as the manufacturing department was concerned about maintaining enough clearance to the rectangular pipe extensions. They preferred a simple notch at the bottom of the panel. They also preferred a simple round hole." (Courtesy Milt Antonick)

This is the initial clay for the Barracuda hood, but the V-shaped scoop was not robust enough so the design developed into the dual scoop shown in the previous photo. The chart Pac tape you see on the clay represents the edge of the part, which was modified to allow sheet metal formation. The actual die-cast part was two-piece, which included a removable 'grille.' The scoop could become functional if holes were cut in the sheet metal. It was never tested by the factory, but the designers doubted that it would have provided sufficient air volume. It is possible to see in this snapshot that the hoods were designed 'off body' on a separate table and then married up at a later date, because of the difficulty reaching across the model. This avoided repetitive back strain. The older A-body Barracuda had been narrow enough to allow hood detailing on the clay. (Courtesy Milt Antonick)

This shot was also taken in 1967 and shows how the rear light panel might look. The lights went unchanged from what you see here, but work on the panel texture continued. (Courtesy Milt Antonick)

Dodge Challenger & Plymouth Barracuda

These two images, although of poor quality, are significant. The top image shows how the Barracuda had developed to the point that it is recognisable as an E-body car. The theme resulted from a weekend spent with Elwood Engle working with Nick O'Shea, Roy Tobias and Milt Antonick.
The bottom photo is the modification made to the same clay model by John Herlitz. His contribution was the minor surface modification released for production, hence his claim to having designed the E-series Barracuda. The rear quarter 'shoulder blade' form was retained but a front fender offset located 4in below the fender peak was eliminated, and the front fender profile given a more dramatic break, more in character with the rear quarter. According to Antonick, the form influence came from the 1967 Cadillac Eldorado. (Courtesy Milt Antonick)

No shrinking violet – 1970

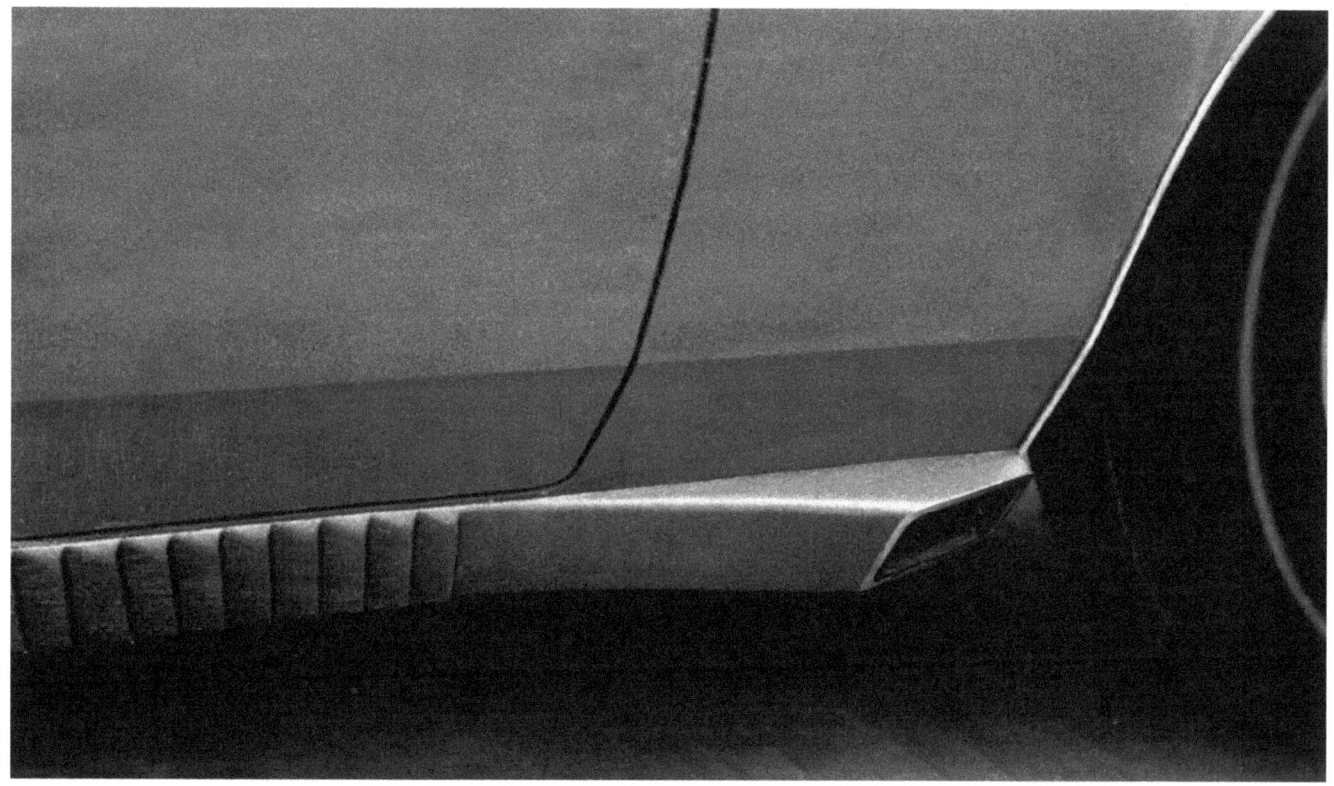

The lower sill molding went almost unchanged on the Barracuda except for deletion of the intended side exhaust exits seen here on the clay model. (Courtesy Milt Antonick)

into the Charger front end. Flanked by exposed headlamps, the gas turbine grille featured a camera bellows-inspired frame that led to a deeply recessed open egg crate. Although the Turbine project was dropped due to the Chrysler fifth generation turbine failing to meet governmental emissions standards, Cameron's work was not in vain. When it came time to design the grille for the 1970 Challenger, the bellows design from the turbine Charger was successfully resurrected, intact, for Dodge's first pony car.

Cameron joined Chrysler in October 1962 after being made redundant from Ford. He would stay over thirty years, during which time he would work in nearly every studio including advanced, pre-production and production exteriors; advanced, pre-production and production interiors; and product identity (nameplates and badges). Sadly he died in 2006, but he will be best remembered for his design of the 1966 Charger and the 1966 Dart.

He liked to begin his mornings, often arriving late, with a "sugar rush" consisting of a candy bar and a Coke. When he sketched, his tongue hung out of his mouth, moving in conjunctive concentration with his Prisma-color pencil. Fellow Dodge stylist Jeff Godshall recalls "We used to kid Carl that if he could have attached a pencil to his tongue, he could have sketched twice as fast."

Besides superficial details like differing headlight and grille arrangements (the Barracuda had two headlights, the Challenger came with four), there was one significant difference between the Plymouth and Dodge versions of the E-body: the Dodge was bigger. The two basic designs had been made up to full-size clays and placed in the Paddock, an area where all designers from every studio could look at other teams' work, and it was immediately apparent that the cars were almost identical. This was not what Dodge boss Robert McCurry wanted – Dodge traditionally had larger

Dodge Challenger & Plymouth Barracuda

cars than Plymouth, and so after checking with the engineers, he told the Dodge studio designers to change it. They made it longer and wider, flaring out the character line that followed the silhouette of the car, exaggerating the smooth 'Coke bottle' design. The end result was a very similar looking car, but the Barracuda utilised a 108in wheelbase and measured 186.7in overall, while the Challenger had a 110in wheelbase and stretched out to 191.3in. This decision to make the Challenger larger, hence more expensive and heavier, would cause controversy for years to come. Regardless, both cars were big, substantially larger and wider than the preceding Barracuda, and bigger than their rivals too.

1970 Barracuda

The engineers and designers had met their goal: both cars were large enough to accommodate the biggest engines that Chrysler had to offer. Standard issue in the Plymouth Barracuda was still the 145bhp 225in^3 straight six, with the base V8 being the 230bhp 318. From there on in you could tick the box on the options list for any V8 offered starting with the 340, then three types of 383 and onto the 426 Hemi and mighty 440. Dodge's Challenger offered the same selection.

The new bodies were built using Chrysler's uni-body technique, and featured torsion bar suspension up front, enhanced with independent lateral non-parallel control arms with Oriflow shock absorbers and a 0.92in anti-roll bar for stability. The rear of the car had a live rear axle held in position by semi-elliptical left springs. An oddity with the larger

1970 'Cuda 440. This numbers-matching 1970 'Cuda has the 440 engine mated to a Torqueflite automatic transmission. The 440 was the largest engine available in any pony car of the time. Plymouth dubbed its offering the 440 Super Commando or 440 Six Barrel, depending on manifold and carb setup. The Six Barrel version was able to beat even the 426 Hemi cars through the quarter mile. At the rear of this 'Cuda is a 8¾ Sure Grip w/3:23. (Courtesy David Castine)

The Elastomeric Urethane bumper was optional in 1970, and was made by molding high-density urethane foam over a standard steel bumper, which was then painted in one of eight body-colors. This 'Elastomeric' bumper was far cheaper to produce than a full urethane bumper as seen on the Pontiac GTO, and had the added bonus of being available for the rear of the car as well, although only in red. This became a popular option above the standard chrome bumpers and always came with body-colored side mirrors. This view of the front of a 'Cuda 440 also shows the side/turning lamps hidden under the curve of the hood lip. The grille itself was finished in Argent Silver. (Courtesy David Castine)

NO SHRINKING VIOLET – 1970

1970 'Cuda 440. The car was ordered fully loaded and comes with air conditioning, AM-FM radio, Elastomeric urethane bumper, luggage rack, power windows, cruise control, Rim Blow horn, hood pins and leather interior. The hockeystick decal (code V6X) seen here was only available in black and initially only found on 'Cudas, but by 1 May 1970, it was available to all Barracudas, becoming the most popular decal for that year. (Courtesy David Castine)

engined cars was that they came with five full leaves and two half leaves on the right, while the left side carried six full leaves. This was to enable control of the extra available torque and reduce axle wind up. The big block cars also came with a larger diameter (0.94in) anti-roll bar at the front.

In the Plymouth studio, it was hoped to offer the Barracuda with body-color urethane bumpers as seen on the Pontiac GTO, but development in this new material was slow and expensive. Designer Milt Antonick said "We couldn't get the funding for the full urethane bumpers so we kind of cheated a little. We molded high-density urethane foam over a standard steel bumper then painted it body-color. It looked great." This 'Elastomeric' bumper was far cheaper to produce than a full urethane bumper, and had the added bonus of being available for the rear of the car as well as the front. This became a popular option above the standard chrome bumpers, and always came with body-colored side mirrors.

The all-steel Barracuda body was based on two different body configurations – a BH23 hardtop coupe and a reinforced BH27 convertible – as was the Challenger. The Dodge, however, offered more brightwork to give it that slightly upmarket look. The Barracuda was also available as a coupe version with fixed rear quarter lights; the order code for this was BL21, but when the cars were built they were given BH23 VIN prefixes with the A93 accessories group code.

Under the long, low hood of the Barracuda sat a deeply recessed grille with an Argent Silver surround that held the single headlamps and inset indicators split by a large central divide. Below the front bumper sat a wide air-intake mouth mounted with two round fog lamps which came as standard fitment on sport models. Optional on all performance versions of the Barracuda and Challenger were the sporty NASCAR-type hood pins, with plastic coated wire protecting the paintwork, leading to the grille. These were in addition to the regular hood latches, rather than a replacement for them.

The rear of the Barracuda was a slightly recessed rectangle made up partly by the rear fenders and

The chrome luggage rack was another popular option but could not be had with the rear spoiler.

This 1970 'Cuda is finished in FJ5 Lime Light and has the optional black vinyl roof and Rallye road wheels. The large chrome road lamps below the front bumper were standard on the 'Cuda model for 1970.

the integrated rear bumper. The recess was painted matt black on 'Cuda models, body-color for base Barracudas, and Argent on the Gran Coupe. The blacked-out tail recess was also given when the A22 (front and rear Elastomeric bumpers) was ordered, regardless of model. The recess held the rectangular, triple-stacked taillights, number plate mount, name badge and trunk lock, the latter two items being set to the right of the number plate mount. Although the Barracuda had championed the large, sporty gas filler cap in previous years, and had been adopted by Dodge for its Charger and new Challenger, the E-body Barracuda fuel filler cap was now hidden behind the licence plate. Keeping with the theme, rectangular exhaust mounts exited through the lower rear valance on the sportier 'Cuda models.

Along the side of the car, the sills were covered in a grooved, gill-like plate that stretched between the two wheelarches. To meet federal regulations, matching, thin oblong reflectors were set on the lower front and rear flanks, red at the rear, amber at the front, and as with all Chrysler Corporation cars of that era, a small, chrome Pentastar was to be found at the bottom of the right front fender. Both cars used Chrysler's 'pull-up' flush-fitting door handles to help give a smooth, uncluttered look, but they were also touted as a safety feature because they were less likely to open in a roll-over situation.

Detail of the 1970 Barracuda rear taillamps. The tail of the car was done by Milt Antonick while the front was carried out by John Herlitz. The outer part of the lights are stop/turn signals, with the reversing lights positioned on the inner side.

Barracudas came in three basic series: the base Barracuda, Gran Coupe, and the 'Cuda. The Gran Coupe was by far the most luxurious model, offering an overhead console integrated into a formed headliner, pedal trim, leather or hound's-tooth cloth and vinyl upholstery, wheel lip and belt moldings, and unique Gran Coupe ornamentation, over and above the standard items in the base Barracuda. The Gran Coupe could be had as either a 2-door hardtop coupe (BP23) or convertible (BP27). Exterior paint was shared with the Challenger, although names were changed, and came in eighteen attention-grabbing shades.

'CUDA

The Formula S was dropped for 1970, but as with the previous year, all performance versions of the Barracuda were dubbed 'Cuda and matched the new Challenger R/T models. They came with many things offered on the Gran Coupe, along with heavy-duty suspension, special 'Cuda ornamentation, F70 x 14 white letter tires, and a 383in^3 V8 fitted with the 4-barrel Carter carb. At no extra cost, wise purchasers could also have the high-revving 340in^3 V8 for great driveability. For the added cost of $871.45, buyers could opt for the concrete-crushing 426 Street Hemi. Because of the extra dollars involved, and

Dodge Challenger & Plymouth Barracuda

The 'hockey stick' decal proved the most popular choice of decal in 1970, and held a call-out for the chosen powerplant. It was only available in black, although alternative colors have been made by aftermarket companies.

the knowledge that the 440 and 340 Six-Barrel could out-accelerate the Hemi 'Cuda, it is no surprise that very few were sold. Only 12 convertibles were ordered with a Hemi, plus two more that were used by Chrysler's press fleet, and only 652 coupe buyers opted for this now sought-after option. When box E74 was ticked on the order sheet, Hemi 'Cuda name tags were added to the car. Base list price for a standard 'Cuda coupe was $3164, while the convertible ran to $3433.

No shrinking violet – 1970

The 1970 'Cuda was available with two 383 V8s: a two-barrel version that put out 290bhp and the larger Super Commando 383 engine that offered 335bhp from its 4-barrel configuration. As seen here, the 4-barrel was topped by a round, unsilenced, dual-snorkel air cleaner finished in black crackle paint. Base 383s were painted Chrysler Medium Blue while the high-performance version came in Street Hemi Orange.

RAPID TRANSIT SYSTEM AND SCAT PACK

In 1968, Dodge created the Scat Pack. It was a line up of all of its performance cars advertised under one banner as a specific group. The group used the logo of a racing bumble bee, while all qualifying cars proudly wore twin bumble bee stripes on their tails. But the Scat Pack was also a regular club, complete with a quarterly newsletter. Members also received a wallet card, jacket patch, bumper sticker, a forty page guide to auto racing, the monthly *Dodge Performance News*, and the quarterly *Dodge Scat News*. Dodge made the *Direct Connection* parts catalogue available to members at no cost, and set up 'Scat packages' of Mopar parts. These included the Showboat (dress up kit), Read-Out (gauges), Kruncher (drag/strip), Bee-Liever (manifold, carb, cam, headers), and Top Eliminator (Six Pak setup, electronic ignition). The total cost of membership was an incredibly low $3 per year on average, and the club ran until the end of 1971.

In 1970 Plymouth introduced the Rapid Transit System, based on Dodge's Scat Pack, reaching out for Plymouth performance fans of all ages. It launched an entire line of economy performance cars aimed at the performance-minded, budget-conscious car buyer. Each member of the Rapid Transit System family featured unique characteristics, but they all flew under the flag of budget performance. Run by ex-drag racer Bill Moeller at Promotions, Inc, Plymouth's RTS matched Dodge with merchandise including pins, jackets, patches and ties to help create a club-like atmosphere. The RTS Caravan was another key ingredient, travelling cross-country with custom-painted street cars, entertaining audiences. The Scat Pack and Rapid Transit System used the attraction of high profile racers like Sox & Martin and Don Grotheer to draw in members, but it was a two way street, as the racers passed on genuine tips on how to get the maximum results from Chrysler's cars in their supercar clinics. The following is an excerpt from the 1970 RTS brochure.

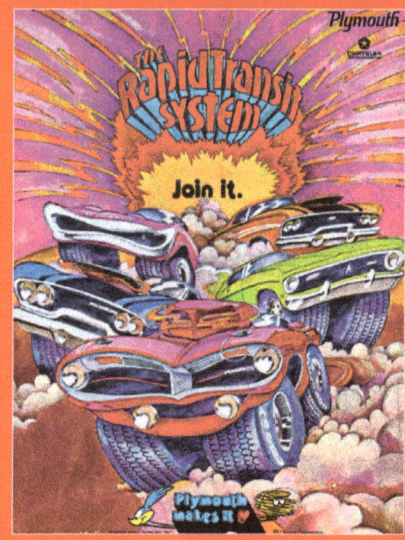

Anybody can offer a car. Only Plymouth offers a system. The Rapid Transit System was the collective name for Plymouth's high performance vehicles and included the 'Cuda, Road Runner, Valiant Duster 340, Plymouth GTX, and the Sport Fury GT.

"Those of us at Plymouth who design and build high-performance cars have been inspired to go beyond just offering cars with big engines, good suspensions, great brakes and fat tires.

We now have a System. An integrated program. It's Mathematics rather than numbers. Oceanography rather than salt water. It's a total concept in high-performance transportation which combines the lessons learned in competition, an information network, people who understand high-performance, trick parts and great products.

The Rapid Transit System is years of racing experience – at Daytona, Indianapolis, Riverside, Irwindale, Cecil County. It's the race cars themselves – drag racing cars, Grand National stackers, rally and Championship cars. And it's the input (and output) gained from all this racing.

The Rapid Transit System is information – the straight scoop from us to you – on how to tune and modify your car, which equipment to use, and how to set the whole thing up for racing. (The subject matter covers everything from this high-performance car catalogue, to Supercar Clinics, to Road Runner decals, to tips on full-race Hemis.) See your dealer or write the Rapid Transit System, P.O. Box 7749, Detroit, Michigan 48207.

The System is people. People like yourself who like cars.

The System is high-performance parts – special cams, manifolds, pistons, bearings, etc. – which are

Each one of the five RTS cars was featured in the 1970 brochure and a red Hemi 'Cuda was shown in the pony car section. The text praises the virtues of the suspension and various engine options and offers advice on which one to choose.

The eye-catching Rapid Transit System brochure advertised options and performance accessories.

now more readily available through parts centers strategically located across the country.

The System is even a piece of the action for beginners. Let's say you're still a few years away from a driver's license, but that hasn't dampened your enthusiasm for cars. Your favorite cartoon is Road Runner, your favorite car is Road Runner, and you only wish your driveway were a couple of miles long. Well, maybe you're not old enough to drive, but you sure can wear a Plymouth racing jacket. And you can also pick up or send for a handful of our decals, stickers, catalogues and brochures. And go to free Sox & Martin or Don Grotheer Super Car Clinics.

Above all, the RTS is the product, Everything from a "sleeper" Duster with a 340in^3 V8, to a giant 440in^3 Sport Fury GT, all the way up to a Hemi-'Cuda with a Quivering Exposed Cold Air Grabber.

And, in between, there are Road Runners and GTXs available with 6-barrel carburetion, and vacuum-controlled induction systems. And 'Cudas with light-weight, high-winding 340 V8s. Each one is a complete high-performance car. With suspension, brakes, driveline and tires to match. (The system doesn't allow for a car that won't corner or stop or stand up under the strain when you stand on it.)

Finally, the Rapid Transit System is common sense on your part. You know when you want to really turn it on, turn it on at a sanctioned strip.

This year, give the Rapid Transit System careful consideration.

Compare it with mere cars. And, if you come to the conclusion you can't beat it – join it."

Don Grotheer was one of Plymouth's favoured drivers. By 1970 he was holding performance clinics along with Sox & Martin for the division.

Sox & Martin held performance clinics at pre-arranged venues for Dodge owners. This is the cover of one of the handouts that it distributed.

With the introduction of the new E-bodied cars the R/T (Road and Track) replaced the Formula S. Available as a hardtop coupe or convertible, the R/T model offered heavy-duty suspension, anti-sway bar, performance hood, Rallye instrument cluster with tachometer, electric clock, and high-performance tires. The black paint on the power bulge hood was an option.

1970 Challenger

The Challenger was a more sophisticated affair and as mentioned, made more use of brightwork. The black front grille (black on R/T and T/A models, Argent Silver on the others) was recessed several inches back from the nose of the car, and was a rounded rectangle holding a mesh insert with twin circular headlamps on either side. The grille area was judged to be barely sufficient for adequate cooling so the headlamp area of the grille was tilted inwards to funnel air through the mesh. This was augmented by the large opening in the lower valance that also directed cool air towards the radiator. The lower front valance also held large round side/turn signal lights molded into the far sides. This opening, as with the grille itself, the mesh insert and headlamps, was surrounded by a thin strip of brightwork. The Challenger name tag sat on the right-hand side of the mesh part of the grille.

The Challenger utilised a similar front bumper to its sister, but due to the extra girth it sat more snugly in the body, with a matching recess in the front panels to allow a neat fit. The rear of the car had similar cutaways from the body to allow a molded look for

That beautiful silhouette was created over a weekend by Dodge studio manager Bill Brownlie in conjunction with designers Carl Cameron and Bob Gale. They worked on several concepts before deciding on the final raised rear deck design suggested by Engle and Herlitz, giving the car that classic 'Coke bottle' shape.

The reversing lamp was the central part of the rear light cluster that stretched the entire width of the rear valance, and this was the first time that a name badge had been placed on top of a reversing lamp. Everybody in the studio was pleasantly surprised when it met state lighting standards.

the rear bumper. Designed by Carl Cameron, the rear lights stretched across the whole width of the car, with all but the central portion in red. The name Dodge sat in chrome letters atop of the clear centre piece that held the back-up light. This was the first

Dodge Challenger & Plymouth Barracuda

The 383 Magnum fitted with a single 4-barrel carb was the standard engine for the R/T model, as shown in this example, although upgrades of a 440 with a 4-barrel or Six Pak, or the 426 Hemi could be ordered. This car has power brakes and variable speed wipers. The battery is an aftermarket replacement.

time that a name badge had been placed on top of a reversing lamp, and everybody was surprised when it met state lighting standards. The trunk lock was centralised and was placed just above the Dodge letters, and the Challenger nameplate was positioned on the right of the trunk lid.

With V8-powered cars fitted with a twin exhaust system, four smaller rectangle exhaust pipes exited below the rear valance, not through it as with the Barracuda. Another tell-tale difference with the cars was the wheelarches. The Dodge had rounded openings at the top that kicked in before forming

NO SHRINKING VIOLET – 1970

All Challengers shared the same script badge held on the right-hand side of the meshed grille, but an additional red-painted R/T badge distinguished this as the performance model. Bodyside stripes with an R/T call-out were also part of the deal.

the wheel lip, whereas the Barracuda's were flat at the top and did not flare out. The Challenger had to carry the mandatory side markers too, but these were more inverted trapezoids than rectangular and came with a bright surround.

Not commonly known, a Challenger could be fitted with one of three different front fenders, depending on choice of engine and wheel selection. One of them was the Hemi fender which had a pronounced rolled under upper lip that helped with clearance for the larger F60 x 15 tires. The filler cap was placed on the passenger side of

Dodge Challenger & Plymouth Barracuda

This Challenger has the 14 x 5.5 deluxe road wheels that would have originally been fitted with Goodyear F70 x 14 fibreglass belted black sidewall tires with raised white lettering.

the car because studio chief Bill Brownlie thought it would be safer to refuel away from traffic if you ran out of fuel. As an option, buyers could have a pop-open sports filler cap with inner locking cap on their Challenger, instead of the standard flush fitting body-colored twist cap.

The Challenger commenced production on 1 August 1969, and was launched to the public on 23 September 1969. It came in two series with four models: the base Challenger series and sportier R/T (Road & Track) series, which included the Challenger hardtop, Challenger convertible, Challenger SE and later Challenger Coupe. Except for the convertibles, which were all produced at the Dodge Hamtramck

Another 383 V8-powered R/T with black vinyl roof and black interior, though this restored example is finished in Plum Crazy and has a single color hood with tie-down pins.

plant in Michigan, production of the SE and hardtops was shared with the Los Angeles, California plant.

The base Challenger was fitted with Chrysler's robust slant six, or could be had with a 340in^3 V8, and was available as either a convertible JH27 or 2-door hardtop (JH23). The more muscular R/T model used the same two bodies, but coded as

Under the hood is a restored 383 Magnum V8 with the correct crackle-finish black paint on the twin snorkel air filter, topped by a Hemi Orange identity plate.

An option on any hardtop Challenger (except 340 cars (A66) and T/As (A53)) was the Special Edition or SE package. This view of a 440-powered 1970 R/T shows the formal rear windscreen designed by Mack King. The mandatory vinyl roof covered the filler bodywork and could be had in white, black, green and Gator Grain (marbled black-brown). This lovely Challenger is finished in Plum Crazy which looks great with the white Boar Grain top and white R/T bodyside stripe. The vinyl roof had a center section that measured 51in between the seams, giving it a very distinctive look and the illusion of a lower roof line.

JS27 for the soft-top and JS23 for the hardtop. The R/T came with a 383 four-barrel, as standard, with optional 440 four-barrel or six-pack and the 426 Hemi. The R/T also came with a Rallye instrument cluster, including a tachometer, an electric clock, heavy-duty suspension and high-performance F70 x 14 white letter tires.

Both the R/T and base versions could be ordered as a luxury Special Edition (SE) model, coded as JS29 for the R/T and JH29 for the standard car. The SE model came with a black, white or green un-padded Boars grain vinyl roof, and a more formal Mack King-designed rear window that was much smaller than the standard fitment. A more unusual Boars grain Antique Green vinyl roof was available with green body-colored cars or green or white interior (optional on other body-colors). An even more unusual choice was the marbled brown and

Another 440-powered Challenger R/T, but this time painted in EB3 Light Blue Metallic with Bright Blue interior. Again, this car has a white roof and matching white R/T bodyside stripe. The new Barracuda and Challenger were 5in wider than the second generation B-body cars, and wider than Ford's Mustang and the Chevrolet Camaro. In the developmental stage the Dodge car went by various names, including Eliminator, Conquest and Explorer, before Challenger was decided upon.

black Gator grain roof that simulated alligator hide, available on a variety of colored vehicles and interiors.

As well as the vinyl roof, a more luxurious interior and special exterior badging made the SE stand out from other Challengers. The SE was only available with the 2-door hardtop body. Padded vinyl roofs were offered on all other hardtop models in the same four color options. A sliding sunroof (code M51) was available on the Challengers, but had to be ordered with the vinyl roof, which covered the cutout.

Transmission options started with a 3-speed A-230 manual gearbox with the selector fitted to the floor, a 4-speed A-833 manual box, also mounted to the floor, and the 3-speed Torqueflite automatic. Cars fitted with the slant six or small-block LA V8s came with the A-903 manual 3-speed or A-904-G Torqueflite, while larger engines were fitted with the more powerful A-727 version, which could be mounted on

Dodge Challenger & Plymouth Barracuda

The interiors on the 1970 challengers were available in Black, Bright Blue, Dark Green, Burnt Orange, Red and Dark Tan and were made in either Regal or Coachman Grain vinyl. Extra cost vinyl seats with fabric inserts were available, but only in four colors. The immaculate interior on this R/T is done in Bright Blue, including the dash, door panels and optional centre console, and also has the wood-grain steering wheel and wood appliqués on the instrument cluster, console and door panels. The blue interior came with matching blue carpet.

There were two versions of the mighty RB 440 V8 in 1970. One used a trio of Holley 2300 twin carbs and was called the 440 Six Pak. This gave out a gut-wrenching 390hp. The other engine was the 440 Magnum seen here. Fitted with a single 4-barrel Carter AVS carburettor and topped by a twin snorkel air cleaner, it gave out 375bhp. Both 440s were painted in Hemi Orange and were available in the 'Cuda too, but were then called 440 Six Barrel (390bhp version) and 440 Super Commando (375bhp version).

the transmission tunnel or on the steering column. The 4-speed manual transmission came with a Hurst wooden pistol-grip shifter as standard, and had a reverse warning light fitted on the dash between the ashtray and glovebox. This transmission was not available to buyers who opted for the base straight-six or 2-barrel 383 V8.

The transmissions were linked to one of three live rear axles, and were identifiable by the diameter of the ring gear. The standard axle fitted to the low performance cars was a 7.25in geared axle fitted with either 2.76:1 or 3.23:1 ratios. Higher performance engines used an 8.75in unit with optional 'Sure Grip' limited slip gears ranging from 2.76:1 up to 3.91:1. Hemi-powered cars fitted with a manual gearbox came with a huge 9.75in Dana 60 Sure Grip axle as standard. Two gear ratios were available: 3.54:1 and 4.10:1. The Dana 60 was also an option on the Hemi automatic and 440-powered cars.

The interior of the 1970 Challenger was well furnished, even in the base model. All Challengers came with contoured, high-backed bucket seats with integrated head-restraints. Vinyl was standard – although vinyl with fabric inserts – and leather was on the options list. Also available as an option was a full-width bench seat covered in vinyl, complete with a central folding armrest. Picking this option limited the buyer to a column-mounted automatic transmission, as there was no place to situate a floor-shifter. All models could be had with 6-way manually-operated front bucket seats.

Door panels were molded ABS plastic that held a woodgrain trim panel with a Dodge Tri-star badge at its centre. This insert was not fitted to early Challengers except the SE. However, the SE package replaced the Tri-star badge with an SE badge, and also saw color-coded carpeting on the lower portion of the door panels to match the floor carpeting. Door carpeting was not limited to the SE though – any Challenger ordered with cloth or leather inserts in the seating would get them, along with rear-seat ashtrays.

The woodgrain insert was not available on the Challenger coupes. A neat, preformed, asymmetrical centre console gave the car a cockpit feel to it, and held the floor-mounted gear selector. Usually fitted in black vinyl, the console came in a variety of colors depending on the choice of interior color selected by the buyer. The instrument panel was color-coded to the rest of the interior, with the upper dash being padded on all models. A Challenger name bar was located to the far right near the A-pillar. The instrument cluster was finished in textured black and held a large 120mph speedometer, and three smaller gauges: fuel, engine temperature and alternator. A fourth pod held a clock, available from the options catalogue.

To the left of the speedo sat switches for headlamps, wipers, and the dimmer. If the optional power-operated soft-top retraction was chosen on the convertible models, then a fourth switch would be placed in this area too. A Rallye dash came standard on all R/Ts, or could be ordered on other models for $90.30. This dash was finished with a woodgrain look, and used four large dials holding a 150mph speedometer, a clock, and an 8000rpm tachometer, as well as the fuel, oil and temperature gauges. The woodgrain appliqué could also be ordered as an option on the standard dash.

The standard steering wheel was a 3-spoke woodgrained affair with a plastic centre holding the horn. Also available was a woodgrain wheel with partial horn ring, an all-plastic steering wheel and a Rim Blow wheel, which had three recessed metal spokes. The Rim Blow was a great idea that didn't work in practice. Underneath the soft grip wheel was a plastic tube that ran around the circumference of the grip. The horn could be blown just by squeezing the plastic tube under the driver's fingers. In reality, though, when the driver was gripping the wheel firmly and changing gear with the other hand, they were likely to sound the horn, too. It also proved to be less robust than was anticipated, so was dropped after two years. A plain smooth black steering wheel was fitted to the mid-season coupes.

The collapsible steering column was covered in a color-coded metal concertina cover. Safety wise, as well as the collapsible steering column and padded dash, the Challenger and Barracuda had integral two-piece door impact beams, and a box section roll-bar for roll-over protection. A useful fitment was the roof-mounted console that held 'low fuel', 'door ajar' and 'seatbelt unfastened' indicators. The console was part of the SE package, but was also used on the Plymouth Gran Coupe hardtops, or any Barracuda or 'Cuda with a leather interior.

The Challenger R/T convertible was the flagship pony car for Dodge. Costing $3535, only 1070 soft-top Challengers were built this year, and all came with a power hood.

Pick a flavour.

The new Chrysler pony cars were made to dazzle and even intimidate competitors. Eighteen eye-popping acrylic enamel colors were available by the end of the year for the Challenger and Barracuda: thirteen standard colors and five optional 'high-performance' or 'high-impact' paints.

Code	Challenger	Barracuda
EB3	Light Blue Metallic	Ice Blue Metallic
EB5	Bright Blue Metallic	Blue Fire Metallic
EB7	Dark Blue Metallic	Jamaica Blue Metallic
FE5	Rallye Red	Rallye Red
FF4	Light Green Metallic	Lime Green Metallic
EF8	Dark Green Metallic	Ivy Green Metallic
FK5	Dark Burnt Orange	Deep Burnt Orange Metallic
BL1	Beige	Sandpebble Beige
FT6	Dark Tan Metallic	Burnt Tan Metallic
EW1	White	Alpine White
TX9	Black	Black Velvet
DY3	Cream	Yellow Gold
FY4	Light Gold Metallic	Citron Mist Metallic
Extra cost colors		
FC7	Plum Crazy (Purple)	InViolet Metallic
FJ5	Sublime (Green)	Lime Light
EK2	Go-Mango (Orange)	Vitamin C Orange
EV2	Hemi Orange	Tor-Red
FY1	Banana (Yellow)	Lemon Twist
FM3	Panther Pink	Moulin Rouge
FJ6	Green-Go	Sassy Grass

Color was an important part of the look so Dodge introduced some audacious, eye-catching colors for 1970, with no less than eighteen body-colors, thirteen of which were standard, or for an extra $14.00 another five 'performance' hues. Two-tone paint was an option on hardtop models. Standard colors were Light Blue Metallic EB3, Bright Blue Metallic EB5, Dark Blue Metallic EB7, Rallye Red FE5, Light Green Metallic FF4, Dark Green Metallic EF8, Dark Burnt Orange FK5, Beige BL1, Dark Tan Metallic FT6, White EW1, Black TX9, Cream DY3, and Light Gold Metallic FY4. Extra cost colors were Plum Crazy FC7, Sublime FJ5, Go-Mango EK2, Hemi Orange EV2, and Banana FY1. Three mid-season options of Silver Poly EA4, Panther Pink FM3 and Green-Go FJ6 were offered after 20 February 1970. The first five extra-cost colors particularly commanded attention. EA4 was not generally offered on the E-bodies, although it could be ordered specially, but the special order paint code was then 999 regardless of which hue was chosen.

No shrinking violet – 1970

ENGINE OPTIONS FOR 1970

Option code	Size (in³)	Size (cc)	Type	AKA	Carb	Power (bhp)
B***	198	3245	6 Cyl	Slant six	1 bbl	101
C	225	3688	6 Cyl	Slant six	1 bbl	145
G	318	5212	LA V8	Small block	2 bbl	230
H	340	5573	LA V8	Small block	4 bbl	275
J**	340	5573	LA V8	T/A Six Pak	3 x 2 bbl	290
L	383	6277	B V8	Big block	2 bbl	290
N	383	6277	B V8	Big block	4 bbl	330
N	383	6277	B V8	Magnum	4 bbl	335
R*	426	6982	RB V8	Hemi	2 x 4 bbl	425
U*	440	7212	RB V8	Magnum	4 bbl	375
V*	440	7212	RB V8	Six Pak	3 x 2 bbl	390

***Challenger Deputy only **Challenger T/A only *Challenger R/T only

Engines

With the engineers achieving their goal of making the engine bay large enough for Chrysler's biggest engines, there was an incredible spectrum of power available for purchasers of Challengers and Barracudas. By the end of the year, no less than ten different power plants could be had from various options.

For the economically minded, the introductory engine was the 225in³ version of Chrysler's slant six. Introduced in 1960 for the Valiant (but used in other ChryCo vehicles too), the well-proven 225in³ (3.7-litre) cast-iron version was offering a respectable 225bhp. Later in the year, this same block was the basis for the 198in³ version placed in the A93 Deputy Challenger, and offered 125bhp.

This Challenger travelled from France for the annual Mopar EuroNationals held at Santa Pod Raceway, Northamptonshire in England. The ex-USAAF Podington bomber base from World War Two was an ideal place to set up a drag strip, and was opened in 1966. The EuroNationals meet is the largest Mopar muscle gathering outside of continental USA.

Dodge Challenger & Plymouth Barracuda

Another Challenger R/T gets its front wheels off the blacktop at Santa Pod. Although heavy compared to its competitors, the Challenger has always been popular with drag racers. (Courtesy Tony Oksien)

Dodge thoughtfully introduces the little limousine. Why not? Who ever sa— that everybody who wants a quick, nimble, "won't drive you to the p— house" kind of car is too young to vote? With this idea in mind, Dod— added enough room in the back seat to make it liveable, a formal sma— rear-window hardtop roof, honest-to-goodness real leather facings on t— bucket seats, matching trim on the doors, and a kind of "Look what I— got that you haven't got" overhead consolette with low-fuel, door-ajar, — seat-belt-reminder warning lights.

The vinyl-covered roof and the unobtrusive SE medallion say you pai— little more than the kid down the block. But considering what you get, — not that much more. You have enough choice in the engine and access— department to fill this page, but Dodge thought the pictures were m— important. Full details follow.

Maybe you have never considered a little limousine. Honestly, why n— And why not now? Challenger SE. Author of that new best seller . . . Go— Formal Can Be Fun.

Overhead consolette, with SE models only.   *Special Edition crest.*

SE for the formal type.

No shrinking violet – 1970

Cover for the Challenger catalogue.

The SE or Special Edition package offered a more luxurious feel to the pony cars and could be had on both the base model and R/T hardtops. Advertised as a miniature limousine, it featured a much smaller formal rear window. The bodywork to fit this was hidden by a compulsory vinyl roof and special window moldings. Inside the car the door panels had woodgrain inserts and SE badging, with matching woodgrain on the instrument cluster. The SE also came with a roof-mounted consolette that warned of doors being ajar, seat belt reminder and low fuel.

Both engines were painted in Chrysler Engine Medium Blue.

The base V8 was the small block 318, based on the LA engine series introduced in 1964 as a 273in^3 V8. Again painted in Medium Blue, by 1970 it was kicking out 230 horses helped by its 2-barrel BBD Carter carb, which offered acceptable acceleration, but by then was not considered to be a performance engine. Another LA V8 was offered in 1970, built as a performance engine. The larger 340 came in two guises, initially fitted with a 4-barrel carburettor and offering 275bhp, and the mid-season 290bhp version that used three 2-barrel Holley carbs on top of a Chrysler-designed Edelbrock manifold. This later motor was fitted to the Challenger T/A and AAR 'Cuda production cars, and was called the 340 Six Pak in the Dodge and 340 Six Barrel in the Plymouth.

As with all of the Challenger and 'Cuda performance engines, the 340 Six Pak was painted Street Hemi Orange and differed from the smaller LA engine in that it had thicker main webs and extra material added around the main bearing area to relieve potential stress. It also had specially machined heads with offset pushrods, allowing for larger ports, offset adjustable, cast-iron rockers, and special rocker shafts. Although officially rated by Chrysler at 290bhp, it is thought that the 340 Six Pak offered nearer 350bhp.

The next engine up was the last of the 1950s big block engines. Introduced in 1958 as either a 350 or 361, the B-block engine was now built as a 383in^3 V8. There were three versions to be found in Chrysler's 1970 Pony cars: a Holley 2-barrel carb version that gave out 290bhp, a high-performance rendering fitted with a single Holley 4-barrel carb, producing 330bhp, and a 383 that gave an extra 5bhp, taking it up to 335bhp. This last engine was

Dodge Challenger & Plymouth Barracuda

This advert for 1970 was used in local and national press, and was drawn by well-known aviation artist Sonny Schug. (Courtesy Brett Snyder)

No shrinking violet – 1970

Arguably one of the most beautiful and sought-after convertibles ever built is the E-body Challenger, and this one is no exception. Finished in FJ5 Sublime, it is a base series car fitted with the optional 340 Four Barrel performance pack, 3-speed automatic transmission, and J54 power bulge hood. The car's build date at the Hamtramck plant in Detroit, MI is 8 April 1970, with the N95-coded Evaporative Emissions Control package, so it is likely it was for sale in California. Although that is the date stated on the SPD (scheduled production date), that is just when Dodge hoped to build the car; there is no way of knowing on which day it was actually built, but they were seldom made on the SPD date. (Courtesy Jim Wilson)

Dodge Challenger & Plymouth Barracuda

The standard black dash on this convertible has a 120mph speedo and no tachometer. The centre console holds the shifter for the automatic transmission.

called the 383 Magnum in the Challenger and 383 Super Commando when fitted in a Barracuda, and was standard issue on the R/T and 'Cuda models. All of the 2-barrel versions were painted blue and were fitted to the JH, BH and BP models, while the 4-barrel engines were finished in Street Hemi Orange and were available on JS and BS cars.

The RB (raised block) engine was based on the same B-block engine, but had a higher deck height which allowed for a longer stroke. These huge engines became the mighty 440in^3 V8s, and in 1970 came in two sizes: a 375bhp mated with a single Carter 4-barrel carb, and the notoriously underrated 390bhp engine that breathed with the help of a

This side view almost exaggerates that classic Coke bottle styling and low slung attitude. The car was ordered with black vinyl interior and black protective bodyside molding to match the black fabric of the soft-top. When stowed in the down position, the power top would have been covered by a black tonneau cover behind the back seats, but it is not present in this picture. (Courtesy Jim Wilson)

The rear of the car wears the J81 'Go-Wing' spoiler with angled ends, bumper guards, and dual exhausts ending in chrome tips. Other items ticked on the order sheet included an AM/FM multiplex standard radio, centre console, and left-hand remote door mirror. (Courtesy Jim Wilson)

Dodge Challenger & Plymouth Barracuda

trio of Holley 2-barrel carbs. For Dodge, the 4-barrel version was known as the 440 Magnum, while the more powerful engine was known as the 440 Six Pak. Plymouth dubbed its offerings the 440 Super Commando and 440 Six Barrel, the latter being able to trounce even the 426 Hemi cars through the quarter mile. Both were painted Street Hemi Orange, and at just $250 for the Six Pak version, this was an absolute bargain for Mopar performance hunters.

The last engine in the arsenal was the legendary 426 Hemi. It was first introduced in 1964 for NASCAR and drag racing use and was not available to the public. On 23 February 1964, three Hemi-powered Plymouth Belvederes overwhelmed the Daytona 500, finishing 1-2-3, with Richard Petty taking his first Super Speedway win in his Plymouth. Jim Paschal came in 5th position in his Hemi-powered Dodge Coronet, followed a few seconds later by Junior Johnson in his Coronet to take 9th place. Further wins followed, and so successful were these new power plants that by 1965 Chrysler was forced by the sanctioning bodies of motorsport to make a choice – either release the Hemi engine to the public for homologation purposes or stop building them altogether.

Because of this, Chrysler had to miss the 1965 race season, but it hadn't given up. Some Plymouth and Dodge B-body cars were already using a 426in^3 Wedge-Head V8, so it made perfect sense to develop this with a Hemi head. For the 1966 model year Chrysler released the Street Hemi as an option in its Plymouth Belvederes and new Dodge Chargers. A year later the engine was made available to mid-size Plymouths and Dodges.

The Street Hemi differed from its racing sister in only a few details: a lower compression ratio, cast-iron instead of aluminium heads, different intake and exhaust manifolds, milder valve timing, and more docile Carter AFBs instead of the race version Holleys. Officially rated at 425bhp, through the quarter mile it could be out-accelerated by smaller, lighter engines, but nothing could touch it for top-end speed.

Until 1970 the 426 had gone mostly unchanged, but that year saw the introduction of hydraulic valve lifters to replace the solid tappets seen in previous Hemis, along with a revised cam. *Road Test* magazine tested a 1970 Challenger R/T fitted with a 426 Hemi, mated to a 4-speed manual transmission and 4.10 Sure Grip differential, for its June 1970 issue. "It takes courage to specify the Hemi option in a Challenger," wrote the editor. "You must face a drivetrain warranty foreshortened to six months, a whopping $1227.50 increase in the $2953 list for a basic Challenger V8 to cover the Hemi and its mandatory related accessories, insurance and operating costs matched by no other US nameplate

A 340 4-barrel fits easily into the expansive engine bay. By the end of the year Dodge and Plymouth were offering ten engine options for use in E-body cars. The 340 remained one of the best choices for a blend of practicality, driveability and performance.

This 1970 Challenger convertible has a substantial black vinyl roof with glass rear window. The V8 convertible cost an extra $347 over the price of a basic hardtop with a six. Bargain!

Close-up of the stylish but impractical Go-Wing. It was fitted at the factory, but they could be installed at dealerships after delivery. The UK owner of this car has overcome the problem of fitting European amber indicators by hiding them on the underside of the spoiler

Dodge Challenger & Plymouth Barracuda

Underside of the trunk lid shows the robust holding brackets for the Go-Wing rear spoiler and correct jacking instructions.

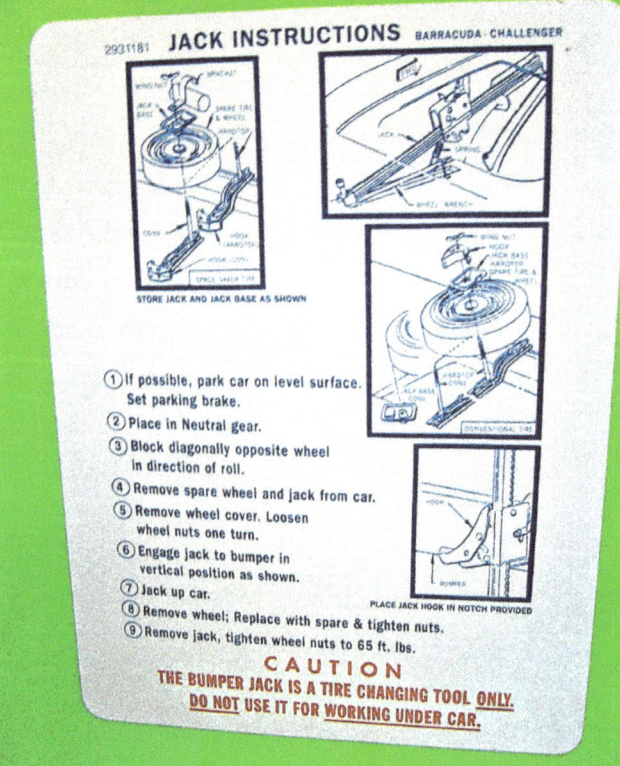

Pristine jacking instructions stuck to the inside of the trunk lid.

except maybe a Hemi Plymouth and the certainty that no fuzz will let you pass by unnoticed. In return, you get power that can rattle dishes in the kitchen when you start it up in the driveway, extra attention in any service station, respect from owners of 428 Fords and SS427 Chevys, a measurable bonus in pride of ownership and immediate status as the car expert on your block." The magazine went on to record a quarter mile ET of 14.0 sec at 104 mph, and summarised: "If brute power over all other considerations is your forte, the Hemi is still boss on the street and if you'll note what most people put under a supercharger in Top Fuel Eliminator, it's boss on the strip as well."

Joe Oldham of *Speed & Supercar* magazine had similar feelings when he drove the first of fourteen Hemi 'Cuda convertibles to come off the production line, one cold Saturday afternoon in late November 1969. Although the Rallye Red 'Cuda constantly leaked transmission fluid from its Torqueflite gearbox, struggled to change up, and even blew out the transmission cooler line, dumping fluid all over the starting line at Raceway Park in Englishtown, New Jersey, Oldham was still favourably impressed with this press fleet car. He noted that the materials used in the bright red interior were the best he had seen from a ChryCo car, the fit and finish were the best he had ever seen in a Mopar, and the

Any Challenger convertible is rare, and to find one fitted with a Hemi is certainly not an everyday occurrence – only nine were built for the domestic US market in 1970. Because of that there have been a whole lot more Hemi convertible clones made in recent years. This car looks factory-fresh, even down to the correct Goodyear polyglass tires. (Courtesy Marc Rozman)

handling was the best he had ever experienced in one, too. High praise indeed from someone who didn't particularly like Mopar products. If the Hemi (or 440) was ordered, it meant the mandatory fitting of other extra cost parts, including larger 11in drum brakes, a larger radiator, two extra half leaves in the right rear spring assembly, the same extra heavy-duty torsion bars, anti-sway bars, spindles, joints and shock absorbers fitted to Plymouth's larger Hemi-powered GTX and

Original badges that sit on the side of the shaker intake can cost hundreds of dollars, if you can find one. (Courtesy Marc Rozman)

Dodge Challenger & Plymouth Barracuda

All Hemi-powered cars had extra strengthening, over and above what a normal soft-top or coupe would have, including a steel plate above the rear axle snubbers. (Courtesy Marc Rozman)

Road Runners, and fat Goodyear E60 Polyglas GT tires mounted on 15 x 7 body-colored steel wheels.

Motor Trend's AB Shuman did a comparison test of the 1970 'Cuda with all three of the big engines. The 440-powered car used a 4-speed manual while the 340 and Hemi used a Torqueflite automatic. The 340 took 6.4 seconds to go from 0 to 60, while the 440 did it in 5.9 seconds and the Hemi in 5.8. Quarter mile times were 14.5 (96mph) for the 340, 14.4 (100mph) for the 440, and 14 seconds (102mph) for the Hemi. Shuman claimed, "From the foregoing, you may have detected a 'slight' preference for the 340 'Cuda. This was intentional. It was the best of the lot!"

Along with the large choice of power plants came an incredible selection of decals and hoods. The base Challenger and Barracuda came with no extra decals and a plain flat hood with no tie-down pins, but most buyers opted for something extra, or received a different variation because of their package or model choice. All Challengers could be ordered with a plain stripe that ran the full length of the car just under the body line. Initially, it could only be had in black, white or red, but later in the year green and blue were offered. After 11 March 1970 it could also be had in chartreuse or magenta. The Challenger could be specified with a painted bumble bee rear stripe, a full-length side stripe with the R/T call-out, a full-length pin-stripe on the JH models, and for the AAR 'Cuda, the unusual strobe stripe. The Challenger T/A used a thicker stripe that started in line with the headlamps and grew wider

1970 Hemi 'Cuda. Although not a separate model, when the Hemi was fitted to the 'Cuda it was badged as a 'Hemi 'Cuda' on the exterior of the car. Plymouth built 652 Hemi Cuda hardtops in 1970, 284 with 4-speed manual transmissions and the remaining 368 with the 3-speed Torqueflite automatic fitted. Only 14 'Cuda convertibles were built, with 2 of those used by Chrysler's press and PR department. This matching-numbers Hemi 'Cuda has the white-over-black interior with the body finished in FC7 InViolet color, two-toned with an EW1 Alpine White roof and color-matching Elastomeric front bumper. It is one of only three two-tone 1970 Hemi 'Cudas known to exist, and the only one in a high-impact color.

This Hemi 'Cuda was built at Hamtramck on 1 Dec 1969 and was ordered with a white on black vinyl interior, high-backed bucket seats, a centre console and a music master AM radio as creature comforts.

before curtailing in line with the back of the rear quarter light. This was reinforced with the 340 Six Pak decal on the front fenders. 'Cudas could also be had with the thin, black, hockey stick shaped decal mounted on the rear flank pronouncing either the 340, 383, Hemi or 440 option. With such an array of decals, it is hard to find two E-bodies that look the same.

Hoods could be chosen that emphasised the muscular torsos of these cars. The long flat hood on the base Challenger held the Tri-star Dodge badge at the front, and emphasised the low-slung look of the car while also managing to hide the windscreen wipers, but on the options list there was the power bulge hood. Designed by Rick Carrell in the Dodge studio, it featured two thin

This Hemi 'Cuda is very well detailed, and even has the seatbelt supports fitted to the roof section.

This Hemi 'Cuda's Rallye dash was not woodgrained, just its centre console, so it came with just a 120mph speedo and no tachometer ...

NO SHRINKING VIOLET – 1970

... though did have a Chrysler Solid State push-button radio.

The stuff of legends: this is the 426 Hemi V8. With a cast iron block, heads and manifold, it was no lightweight, but it did have loads of cubes. Breathing through two Carter AFB 4-barrel carbs, the Street Hemi gave out 425bhp at 5000rpm. Although hard to tune, when it was set up well this race-bred monster had no serious competitors on the track, strip or street. (Courtesy Jim Wilson)

An unusual view: the Hemi, now with its rubber surround and unsilenced aircleaner fitted before attaching the Shaker hood scoop.

air scoops, one on either side of the wide bulge. Body-color was standard, but could be had with the V21 vinyl hood blackout as an accent, and it was deep enough to hold engine identity plates on its side, but if you ticked the painted option it came with a wider bodyside stripe. The power bulge hood also spelled out 'Dodge' on the front lip.

The Challenger T/A came with yet another hood made from fibreglass that featured a raised air scoop, making best use of airflow over the car. Because of the lack of radio suppression available from this hood, the antenna on the T/A was relocated from the right front fender to the right rear quarter panel. The Barracuda's AAR hood was again finished in matt black fibreglass, but it was more nasal-like, and was equipped with four thin air inlets near the windscreen, allowing fresh air into the cockpit when the vents were opened under the dash.

The famous Shaker cold air induction scoop was a popular choice, and came standard with the Hemi engines. This intake, created by Milt Antonick in the Plymouth studio, was not part of the hood at all

Transformation complete. Hemi engines had their own unique way of breathing, through the famous Shaker cold air induction scoop. This intake, created by Milt Antonick in the Plymouth Studio, was not part of the hood at all but sat directly on top of the air filter and peeped through a hole cut into the 'high-performance' hood. When the car was running the intake would vibrate, hence the name Shaker. This was the only intake that was used on both Plymouth and Dodge. It came standard with the Hemi engines, but could be ordered on non-Hemi vehicles too.

All 'Cudas came with heavy-duty suspension as standard, but cars fitted with the 440 or 426 Hemi came with the A727 high-upshift Torqueflight automatic, 0.92in diameter front torsion bars, beefed up rear leaf springs, 0.94in extra heavy-duty front stabiliser, extra heavy-duty shocks, a Dana 60 rear axle and F60 x 15 tires on 7in rims. Even with the larger tires, over-enthusiasm with the accelerator would see the evaporation of the tread. This car was fitted with the optional 4.10:1 ratio axle, power brakes, a pair of racing mirrors, hood pins with lanyards and dual exhaust with chrome tips. (Courtesy Jim Wilson)

No shrinking violet – 1970

This image shows the gill-like lower sill molding minus the side exhaust exits planned in the developmental stage.

and sat directly on top of the carburettors, peeping through a hole cut into the 'high-performance' hood. When the car was running the intake would vibrate, hence the name. This was the only intake that was used on both Plymouth and Dodge and could be ordered on non-Hemi vehicles too. It was only available in Argent Silver or matt black (although a red version could be ordered to match the hood color on 'Cudas), and came with a fuzzy 'Shaker' decal under the hood.

It is sometimes said that the T/A hood was used in place of the Shaker hood because the demand exceeded supply in 1970. However, it was discovered that the extra reinforcement required to support the Challenger Shaker hood was too strong. In a front end collision, the hood could shear the hinge bolts off, sending the hood through the windscreen and into the passenger compartment. They were withdrawn for a few months because of this, and the problem was corrected by adding 'crumple zones' in the under-skin so the hood could buckle on impact.

Not every motoring journalist saw the potential of these cars when they were first released. *Car and Driver* magazine tested a Hemi-powered Challenger in November 1969 and requested that the engineers responsible fall on their swords. It said, "In the flesh it is a highly stylized Camaro with strongly sculptured lines, more tumble-home and grille vaguely in the Charger tradition. There's no doubt it is a handsome car but it also has a massive feeling which is totally unwelcome in a sporty car – a massive feeling which results from a full five inches more width than a Mustang and a need to sign up with Weight Watchers."

But it wasn't just the overall size that bothered the magazine; it went on to slate the weight, handling and visibility. It added, "It's just too heavy. The idea of a 'sporty' car weighing within 100 pounds of a comparably equipped Road Runner or Super Bee is ridiculous ... What has happened is that Chrysler has built itself a 'performance' car that is 300 pounds heavier than a Cobra Jet Mustang and almost as nose-heavy. Nice going, you guys." It also said that of the many Hemi-powered cars it had tested over the years, this was the first that "didn't offer more pleasure than grief. It was very ill at ease in traffic with a tortuous idle when held in drive against the brake and very poor low speed throttle response. Not infrequently it would backfire through the carburettor when coming off idle and, occasionally, after a backfire, die right in the middle of the street." It wasn't best pleased with the SE package either, stating that the consollette was all but useless, and after trying to see through the smaller rear screen, concluding "you no longer see any of the rear deck from the driver's seat and the Challenger consequently becomes a park-by-ear car. In all, the SE package serves to exemplify the entire Challenger approach – lavish execution with no thought to practical application."

It is true that the Challenger and Barracuda were heavy cars, and had definitely left the realm of light,

Dodge Challenger & Plymouth Barracuda

A very straight and original-looking Challenger R/T fitted with the optional 383 4-barrel. It is tastefully finished in FF4 Light Green Metallic with correct black R/T full length body stripe and road wheels. The car currently resides in the United Kingdom, just one of the countries around the world that has a large population of E-bodies.

The interior of the Challenger is well adorned, and comes with a color-keyed centre console holding the optional slapstick gear changer for the automatic transmission, Rallye cluster dash that includes a tachometer, and is covered with a woodgrain appliqué, green vinyl bucket seats, and the woodgrain Rim Blow steering wheel.

The most unusual detail about this Challenger R/T is sometimes missed by the casual observer – it has the optional Gator Grain vinyl roof.

sports car behind. They were now swimming with the big fish in the muscle car class.

Mid-season saw the release of two more Challengers: the A93 Deputy and the A53 T/A. The Deputy package along with a matching Barracuda were launched in March 1970 as price-leader coupes, aimed at the economically minded or frugal buyer. They used a hardtop body, but the retractable rear quarter window was replaced by a fixed window, the rear window winder was removed, and the hole was plugged with a chrome button. The vinyl-covered bench seats were similar to those found in the Barracuda but with a plainer vinyl pattern, available in black or white only, while the car was fitted with a minimal amount of trim.

The steering wheel was similar to the standard woodgrain-style wheel, except that it had a smooth black rim. The Deputy could be had with a unique brighter white vinyl roof as well as the other vinyl options, and came with its own docile and exclusive 198in^3 version of the slant six engine as the standard

NO SHRINKING VIOLET – 1970

Both the AAR 'Cuda and Challenger T/A shared the same 340in³ V8. In the 'Cuda it was known as the 340 Six Barrel and as a 340 Six Pak in the Dodge. The engine featured three in-line, two-barrel Holley carburettors on top of a Chrysler-designed Edelbrock aluminium manifold. The aim was to achieve reasonable fuel economy with exceptional performance when required. While the vehicles were driven lightly, only one of the three carbs would operate, but under heavy acceleration all carbs would kick in. From a standing start these 290hp engines could out-accelerate a Hemi-powered car before the Hemi's superior breathing would win through. The 340 Six Pak in the Challenger T/A was topped by a special oval air filter fitted with a rubber seal to fit the fibreglass air intake on the hood. The engine and air filter were finished in Hemi Orange.

power plant, although the 225, 318 and 383 motors could be ordered from the options list. The A93 coupe had only one horn instead of the usual two, while almost everything else on the deputy was an extra cost item from the options catalogue, including the cigar lighter in the ashtray. Plymouth called its simply the Barracuda coupe, but Dodge called its fixed-window Challenger coupe the 'Deputy' after a sheriff-type character that appeared in Dodge television commercials of the time. Although the coupe was continued the following year, the unique cowboy name was not used in 1971.

Seeing larger crowds attracted to races, with Chevrolet, Ford and AMC all participating, Chrysler decided to have another crack at the SCCA's Trans-Am race series in 1970, so for homologation purposes, it introduced the Challenger T/A to the buying public in the spring of 1970. The T/A, or Trans-Am package for the public, included a special 290bhp 340 Six Pak engine matched to a 4-speed manual transmission and a 3.55:1 ratio rear axle with Sure Grip. A 3.91:1 ratio axle was optional. Easily identifiable from its unique matt black fibreglass hood and T/A side stripes, the hood featured a raised 'pursuit plane' air scoop, and according to the designers at the time, this was borrowed from the 1969 'Cuda and came with hood tie-pins. Other features included special body side exhaust outlets that exited just in front of the rear tires, fat Polyglas GT G60 x 15 tires on the rear, E60 x 15 tires up front, disc brakes, optional dual chin spoilers under the front valence, a black 'ducktail' spoiler mounted on the trunk, and 340 decals just behind the front wheelarch.

The T/A had a pronounced rakish stance, caused by larger tires being fitted to the rear and an increased leaf spring camber to allow clearance for the side exhaust pipes. The interior options were the same as the base Challenger, while the Rallye package, including its heavier duty suspension, was an option, although front and rear anti-sway bars were added along with heavier duty shocks. Performance of the production cars was impressive, with a T/A reaching

The street version of the Challenger T/A was a good seller in the one year it was available. A T/A could reach 60mph in just 6 seconds, 100mph in 14 seconds, and cover the quarter mile in the mid 14s. (Courtesy Marc Rozman)

Dodge Challenger & Plymouth Barracuda

This particular T/A has the standard black rear spoiler but also the rare optional rear window louvers. (Courtesy Marc Rozman)

Unique decals and engine call-out on the front fenders were another feature of the T/A. (Courtesy Marc Rozman)

The AAR Cuda and the Challenger T/A shared the same mechanics, including the side exit exhausts. (Courtesy Marc Rozman)

60mph in just 6 seconds, 100mph in 14 seconds, and covering the quarter mile in the mid 14s. As a mid-year release, sales were impressive at just under 2400 units in the USA and 118 in Canada, but success at the race track was elusive, so once more, Chrysler quit after just one season.

Plymouth also fielded a car for the Trans-Am series based on its E-body car, the A53 body-coded AAR (All American Racing) 'Cuda. Although mechanically identical to the Challenger, even down to the engines, the AAR 'Cuda had several cosmetic differences. A different nasal-type hood scoop, designed by Milt Antonick and developed by Creative Industries (CI), was grafted onto the CI fibreglass hood, and the matt black paint ventured as far as the tops of the front fenders, matching the color of the hood. Once developed, the hoods were produced by Chrysler Canada.

A unique strobe stripe ran along the upper beltline of the car and was tipped by the AAR shield and Cuda logo. Milt Antonick said that the strobe stripes caused problems. "We didn't know how to figure the stripes so that we could make it easy for the manufacturer, 3M, to produce. One of the guys in the studio, Clint Washburn (studio engineer), was great at math, and he calculated a 4 per cent increase in block size from segment to segment."

Both the 'Cuda and Challenger race cars

One of the two Dodge entries in the SCCA Trans-Am racing series was piloted by Sam Posey. His lime green #77 car managed to finish in the top three position several times, but the car was under-developed and had little chance of winning the series. If Chrysler had not withdrawn its support for the next season, it may have been more competitive.

This is Sam Posey at the wheel of his Challenger T/A. The Mopar Trans-Am cars ran 340 V8s, destroked to 303in³ to sneak in under the 5.0-litre limit set by the SCCA. It didn't always finish in one piece! (Courtesy Barry Washington)

So fans could keep up with what was happening throughout the race season, Dodge produced this neat calendar, showing all of the races involving the T/A between April and October 1970.

were built by famed racer Dan Gurney at his All American Racing company – hence the AAR name for Plymouth's 'Cuda – and used special Pete Hutchinson-Keith Black built 460bhp 340ci V8s that were destroked to 305ci to meet SCCA rules. Gurney drove one of the two AAR 'Cudas himself, but it was racer Sam Posey who gained the most success during that season, finishing in 3rd place three times out of the eleven races in his T/A.

The cars were made as light as possible, even going to the extreme of acid dipping the whole body to remove excess metal. Full roll-cages were welded to the floorpan, and the rear axle gained leading lines that helped reduce wheel hop. SCCA rules stated the race cars had to use the same stock block and heads as production models, but the race engines were classed as special editions, and

This is almost as good as it gets. This beautiful numbers-matching AAR 'Cuda looks perfect in its EV-2 Tor Red paintwork, sitting on the jetty near its home in Santa Barbara, California. The production model of the AAR came with a hot 340in³ V8 fitted with three 2-barrel Holley carbs. (Courtesy David Fogg)

Two views of the first AAR 'Cuda hood at the clay model stage. The nasal-type hood scoop was designed by Milt Antonick, but he carried out this work at the company that would build the hoods, Creative Industries (CI). The air intake was grafted into the CI fibreglass hood then painted matt black. The centre section of the scoop was deleted on the final design.

The AAR was named after Dan Gurney's All-American Racing company, the organisation that built the race cars. (Courtesy David Fogg)

NO SHRINKING VIOLET – 1970

This angle shows to great effect the mathematical precision of the side stripes, which increased in size 4 percent from block to block. (Courtesy David Fogg)

The 340 Six Barrel was painted Hemi Orange, along with the airfilter cover. Attention to detail has been lavished on this example, even down to the correct Mopar battery and black-painted upper cowl panel fitted to early 1970 model vehicles. (Courtesy David Fogg)

Neat trunk space fitted with the correct grey carpet and jack mounted to the left fender. Note the Mopar compressed air bottle strapped to the space saver tire. (Courtesy David Fogg)

Cockpit has the Rallye dash, woodgrain steering wheel and matching pistol grip shifter. (Courtesy David Fogg)

Another AAR Cuda, this time painted in Lime Light and wearing the optional extra front fender spoilers. (Courtesy Marc Rozman)

like the production 340s had thicker main webs and extra material added around the main bearing area to relieve potential stress. They also had specially machined heads with offset pushrods, allowing for larger ports, offset-adjustable cast iron rockers, and special rocker shafts. The push rods themselves were longer than the production models'. The end result was that production models fitted with the 340 became the pre-eminent Mopar pony car, maximising the superb balance of power, handling and driveability.

Plymouth managed to sell 2724 of the street version AAR 'Cudas, almost meeting the 2800 required for homologation purposes, but overall sales of the Barracuda were poor, with just 55,499 units built. Plymouth executives had expected a great sales year from the new E-bodies, and were desperately disappointed in what they saw; again, it was the right car at the wrong time.

There was also a special package available through dealers in the Los Angeles and San Francisco areas. Known as the Western Sport Special, this discounted package of options was first seen in 1969 on Dodge Darts, but in mid-December 1969 it was made available on the base 1970 Challenger. Coded A91, it was built in Los Angeles until May 1970, when production of E-bodies ceased in that location; from then on, orders for the WSS were

No shrinking violet – 1970

Plymouth fielded the AAR 'Cuda in the Trans-Am series. This was an out-and-out battle between Ford, General Motors, AMC and Chrysler. Dan Gurney (right) built the race cars for Chrysler, so they were named after his All American Racer company. He drove this #48 car while team-mate Swede Savage (left) drove #42.

Dan Gurney waits in his #48 car while the pit crew undertakes a tire change in the 1970 TransAm race season. As with NASCAR, SCCA Trans American rules allowed only a certain number of crew near the car at any one time. (Courtesy Jeff Bangert, www.transamcuda.com)

processed through the Hamtramck plant. The WSS featured a vinyl roof, woodgrain instrument panel, remote control mirror, a Rim Blow steering wheel, sill and belt moldings, front splash pan scoop, cowl molding, the astrotone applique above the rear taillights, a chrome pedal dress-up kit, bumper guards with rubber inserts, and F78 x 14 inch white side wall tires mounted on 14in Rallye wheels. To identify this special edition, a 'Western Sport Special' decal was mounted high up on both the rear fenders. At just $199.50 this package was great value for money, and it found 1592 buyers, with most (1066) going for the 318 V8 and another 381 going for the big block option of a 383in^3 V8. Being built in California at the Los Angeles plant, all of these Challengers had the N95 Evaporative Emissions Control package, mandatory for all cars sold in that state.

Total sales of the new Challenger were more promising at 83,032 units, with 19,938 being R/Ts, but sales of the now dated Dodge Charger fell by nearly 40,000, with many buyers moving over to

The Ramchargers started out in the early sixties as a club for Chrysler employees that wanted to work on their cars in their spare time, souping them up. The success that some of them achieved at the drag strip prompted Chrysler to help with equipment and development. The Ramchargers (along with Plymouth rivals, the Golden Commandos) became a recognised team and were incredibly successful. By 1970 they were campaigning the new Challenger.

In 1970 Dodge released a special package available only through dealers in the Los Angeles and San Francisco areas. Known as the Western Sport Special, this discounted package of options was first seen in 1969 on Dodge Darts, but in mid-December 1969 it was made available on the base 1970 Challenger. Coded A91, the WSS featured a vinyl roof, woodgrain instrument panel, remote control mirror, a Rim Blow steering wheel, sill and belt moldings, front splash pan scoop, cowl molding, a chrome pedal dress-up kit, bumper guards with rubber inserts, and F78 x 14in white sidewall tires mounted on 14in Rallye wheels.

No shrinking violet – 1970

The Western Sport Special came with unique decals on the rear fenders.

the Challenger. Dodge wanted to take sales from a competitor, not one of its own vehicles. As the year came to a close, it was obvious to anybody who cared to look that sales of performance cars were falling and sales of economy cars, both home-grown and imported, were on the rise. Even Plymouth's lowly Valiant increased sales enough to take that division back to third place in the

Vanishing Point. *It's the maximum trip ... at maximum speed.* The star was plainly the car in this road movie as Kowalski tries to win a bet that he can deliver a car from Colorado to California in just 15 hours. The makers had at their disposal five brand new white Challengers on loan from Chrysler, four fitted with 440 Magnum engines, and one equipped with the standard 383in^3 V8. This last car was used for some interior shots. Although a little worse for wear, all five cars were returned to Chrysler at the end of filming.

Dodge Challenger & Plymouth Barracuda

Although a one-off show car, the Dodge Yellow Jacket of 1970 was not so much a way-out concept car as a sporty evolution of the Challenger – dressed up with a number of Scat Pack features that were available as options on several contemporary Dodge production models. It started life as the first 1970 Hemi Challenger R/T convertible to come off the production line, painted black with a black soft-top, black interior and stripe. It was taken to the Hamtramck executive garage along with the invoice, which read "Custom Challenger Yellow Jacket." Designed by Dodge engineers and built in Dearborn by Synthetex Inc, the Yellow Jacket was finished in Pearlescent Honey Gold with twin contrasting side stripes that flowed along the belt-line to disappear into the air scoops above the rear wheels. Predating today's many 'targa-top' sports car models, the Yellow Jacket had a removable roof panel and integral chrome roll-over bar built into the B-pillars behind the two-seater cockpit. The show car's high-performance image was boosted by four SuperLite headlamps, an air-dam nose spoiler, a Shaker-style air intake, side air scoops, side-mounted exhaust pipes, deeply dished 15in alloy wheels, and a full-width aerodynamic rear wing, which could be raised and lowered electrically via a dashboard switch. The cockpit accommodated twin high-back bucket seats trimmed in black, nestled into a molded rear bulkhead painted to match the exterior body-color. The sporty, open-car feeling could be enhanced by lowering the powered rear window between the B-pillars. Even with the roof on and windows up, a fresh atmosphere could be achieved, thanks to the flow-through ventilation system that extracted stale air via vents in the rear deck. Beneath the sporty exterior, Yellow Jacket was equipped with a selection of Scat Pack hardware to deliver genuine high performance, including a 426in^3 (6980cc) Hemi engine, manual four-speed transmission, heavy-duty suspension and brakes and extra-wide Goodyear tires. This car would undergo yet another transformation when it became the Diamante show car.

manufacturers table, a position it hadn't enjoyed since 1959.

Some of Dodge's later sales success can be traced to the movie *Vanishing Point*. Released in March 1971, actor Barry Newman played Kowalski, a driver hired to take a white 440in^3-powered 1970 Challenger hardtop from Colorado to California in just 15 hours. The drug induced, psychedelic trip that ensues sees the main character storm across the country, chased by the police, picking up gay hitchhikers, meeting a naked girl on a motorcycle and being guided by a blind radio jock called Supersoul, in one of the original road movies. The fiery climax sees Kowalski plough into a police roadblock made up of bulldozers, but sharp-eyed moviegoers soon realised that it is not a Challenger that hits the roadblock. Chrysler had loaned Richard C Sarafian, the director, five white 1970 Challengers and wanted them back, so a derelict 1967 Chevrolet Camaro was purchased from a nearby junkyard and driven into the bulldozers. In 1997 this cult classic film was remade for TV, again starring a 1970 Challenger R/T, but this time fitted with the 426in^3 Hemi V8. The remake also featured a 1968 Charger driven by one of the cops.

A Challenger also featured, along with a Plymouth 'Cuda, in the almost forgotten Gus Trikonis movie *Moonshine County Express* from 1977. A slightly more adult version of the *Dukes of Hazzard* story, three grown-up daughters are left orphaned when their boot-legging father is murdered by a competitor. They take up the business of running moonshine across state borders in high speed chases.

4
THE ULTIMATE PONY CAR – 1971

The writing was on the wall. Chrysler, along with all other motor manufacturers, could see that the muscle car had had its day and future sales were limited. From government pressure, Chrysler was forced to divert money away from product planning into engineering more fuel efficient, safer, and cleaner vehicles. In December of 1970, the Clean Air Act was passed, charging the auto makers to reduce carbon monoxide and hydrocarbon emissions by a staggering 90 per cent by 1975, and a similar reduction in nitrogen oxides by 1976. Insurance premiums, especially for younger drivers, sky-rocketed to unaffordable limits, hitting the largest part of the muscle car market. Consequently, 1971 became the final year for true American-built performance cars.

The Chrysler Corporation made some immediate changes for the new model year. It reduced the choice of engines by dropping the lower-rated 383 4-barrel and the 440 4-barrel V8s, and introduced a second slant six. It very quietly dropped its 5 year/50,000 mile drivetrain warranty and reverted to the previous 12 month/12,000 mile coverage. Dropping out of the SCCA's Trans-Am series meant the loss of the 340 Six Pak engine as the production of the AAR 'Cuda and Challenger T/A ceased.

Following the industry trend, advertised horsepower was now given as net. Traditionally, engines were measured on a dynamometer-tester with no ancillaries attached and an unrestricted exhaust, offering a gross horsepower. From 1971, a more realistic test was carried out following guidelines set down by the Society of Automotive Engineers (SAE), with all belt-driven ancillaries and the exhaust system in place. This slight of hand move instantly reduced advertised horsepower without having to engineer changes. However, Chrysler did

Changes to the body were minimal for 1971, but the Barracuda did receive a substantial facelift that easily identified it from the previous year. This advert was seen in Car and Driver *magazine and shows the very different front grille for the '71 Barracuda. Designed by Milt Antonick, it featured six D-shaped openings, three on each side of the centre bar, and for the first and last time, quad headlamps.*

131

A Lime Light Hemi 'Cuda seen as part of the celebration of the Hemi engine exhibition at the Walter P Chrysler Museum in Detroit. Of the 107 coupes built with a Hemi in 1971, 59 had the 4-speed manual transmission, while 48 came with a tough Torqueflite automatic. This superb car has an Elastomeric color-keyed front bumper, black vinyl roof, chrome luggage rack, the correct Goodyear Polyglas tires, and even a set of indicators on the top of the front fenders as part of the Light package. (Courtesy Chrysler Historical Dept)

reduce compression ratios in all of its engines except the 225in³ slant six, 426 Hemi and the remaining 440.

Flash fish: 1971 Barracuda

Except for a mild face-lift, the basic E-body Barracuda went virtually unchanged for this year. Often dubbed by critics as the 'JC Whitney 'Cuda,' the '71 received many unnecessary, and some might say unfortunate trim changes. Criticism of the plain front grille from the previous year caused an overreaction in the Plymouth studio and the subsequent cheese grater grille seen on the '71. Another Milt Antonick design, it was made up of six D-shaped openings, three on each side, that were supposed to suggest more aggressive Barracuda teeth, but in the end made the front look busy and cramped.

This year saw the only time that the Barracuda wore quad headlamps like its Challenger sister. They sat outside of the fish tooth grille in a grille pan painted Argent Silver or body-color, depending on model selection, and made the grille look even more cluttered. The lower valance that sat below the bumper was more pronounced and had two vertical splits. Added to this were the four simulated air-intake fish 'gills' fitted to the 'Cuda, attached to the front fenders just before the door split. The 'Cuda hood went unchanged but the Barracuda and Gran Coupe hoods received some minor modifications, as did the front bumper. The rear

Another 'Cuda, this time finished in black and fitted with the hefty 440, looking quite restrained with no side decals and plain black road wheels with dog dish caps. This car also has the Light package, as can be seen by the optional fender top indicators and tan interior. The new dummy chrome gills on the front fenders contrast nicely with the dark bodywork. (Courtesy Chrysler Historical Dept)

bumper went unchanged from 1970 until later in the season, when new safety regulations caused both the front and rear bumpers to change slightly. The Plymouth name badge moved from the right of the front grille to the front right side of the hood. Base Barracudas and Gran Coupes could be ordered with the 'Cuda performance hood for just an extra $20.95, while the sporty hood pins added another $15.40 to the bill.

The rear of the car now featured redesigned light bezels that separated the stop and turn signals from the reversing lights. Optional with the spoiler package was a redesigned rear spoiler called a Go-Wing, which came in matt black. Bewildered by the attention lavished on it by the Plymouth designers, *Car and Driver* wrote of the facelift, "One look at the new Barracuda and we can hardly wait till last year."

The most striking change was in the decals offered. There was still a large selection, but by far the most popular was the large matt black billboard decals that covered almost the complete rear flanks. They ended just before the middle of the door, and held an engine call-out. These were standard on the BS23 hardtop coupe 'Cuda and BS27 soft-top 'Cuda, and optional on the other two other series. The base Barracuda was still available as a BH23 hardtop or BH27 convertible, and could still be had as the economy (A93) BH23 coupe too, with its fixed rear quarter light going unchanged. The base Barracuda came with dual horns, day/night interior mirror, left exterior mirror, brake warning light, bucket

Dodge Challenger & Plymouth Barracuda

With fewer sold in 1971 than in 1970, the rarest E-bodies are the Hemi convertibles. Only 11 were built in 1971, and of that number just 7 were built for the US domestic market. Five of the '71 Cuda convertibles had Torqueflite automatic transmission and only 2 had manual shifting. This Hemi 'Cuda clone resides in the UK and looks stunning.

seats, cigarette lighter, heater and defroster, two-speed wipers, hub caps and rubber matting. Color-coded carpeting replaced the rubber mats on hardtops and convertibles.

The more luxurious BP23 Gran Coupe came with all of the above, but also saw the return of the overhead console, a formed headliner, leather bucket seats, pedal trim, anodised aluminium wheel lip and belt moldings, special ornamentation, and a V8 engine. They could now only be ordered as hardtops, with the convertible being dropped. All remaining convertibles came with manual operation as standard, or for extra $48.70 a power system was fitted. This would be the last year ever for Plymouth convertibles.

The flagship 'Cuda offered everything fitted to the two lower-priced models, along with a performance hood, chrome sill moldings, color-coded grille, matt black rear deck panel, heavy-duty suspension, white-letter tires and the 383in^3 V8. As with the previous year the Challenger

The famous Shaker air intake with the rarely seen Hemi 'Cuda badge on the side.

The ultimate pony car – 1971

The massive 'billboard' signage was a popular choice for buyers, but not for the technicians who had to fit them. Taking up most of the rear fender, they had to fit these in one go, around the side marker. Initial wastage was very high until the factory started to use a soap solution on the paint to help application. The styling studios were told never to create anything as large as that again. They were dropped for 1972, although eventually became available in the aftermarket. They came in black or white and also held an engine call-out that read 340, 383, 440, or Hemi when fitted with that engine.

and Barracuda shared the same dash, which went virtually unchanged for 1971.

Again there were eighteen body-colors for this year, twelve standard and six extra-cost high-impact colors. The standard colors were listed as Winchester Gray Metallic GA4, Glacial Blue Metallic GB2, True Blue Metallic GB5, Evening Blue Metallic GB7, Amber Sherwood Metallic GF3, Sherwood Green Metallic GF7, Autumn Bronze Metallic GK6, Tunisian Tan Metallic GT2, Rallye Red FE5, Snow White GW3, Formal Black TX9, Gold Leaf Metallic GY8 and Tawny Gold Metallic GY9. The high-impact colors were In Violet FC7, Sassy Grass Green FJ6, Bahama Yellow EL5, Tor-Red EV2, Curious Yellow GY3 and Lemon Twist FY1.

Added to this was the $82.40 option of a Boar Grain vinyl roof that could be had in either green, black gold or white. The black and white vinyl roof could be had with any color body paint with the exception of Snow White paint with a white vinyl roof. The gold vinyl could be had with gold, black or snow white body paint. Yet another option was the backlight louver package offering a rear window louver, black vinyl roof and a pair of color-coded racing mirrors, all for just 175.05. A chrome luggage rack could also be ordered for the trunk lid but

Although it is a clone, this car has been done very well indeed. The interior is white on black (black dashboard, centre console and carpets) vinyl with a white soft-top and cover. The Rallye dash and centre console have the woodgrain appliqués to match the woodgrain Rim-Blow steering wheel and wooden Hurst pistol-grip shifter. The car also has the pedal dress-up kit and a pair of chrome racing mirrors.

The rear of the car now featured redesigned light bezels that separated the stop and turn signals from the reversing lights. The rear bumper was unchanged from 1970 although, later in the year, larger overriders were used to meet safety regulations. The exhausts on the 'Cuda still exited through the lower rear valance.

The ultimate pony car – 1971

Although the early Barracudas were renowned for their mammoth trunk space, the larger E-body cars had smaller trunks best described as adequate. The space saver wheel helped reduce wasted space, although it was placed in the centre and not to one side, which would have helped even more. The jack can be seen strapped to the left rear panel, while the jacking instructions are pasted to the trunk lid.

could not be had with the spoiler. The Elastomeric front bumpers were still available but now only came in six colors: Bright Blue Met, Avocado, Citron Yella, Plum Crazy, Red and Tor-Red. If both front and rear bumpers were ordered, Bright Blue Met and Avocado were not available.

Power differed little from the previous year, although choice was reduced to eight engines. The base powerplant was the 198in^3 slant six borrowed from the Valiant. This was the standard issue in the BH21 Barracuda coupe and offered 105hp (net). The second slant six was the 225in^3 version that provided 110hp (net). This was the standard engine in the Barracuda hardtop and Gran Coupe, optional on the A93 fixed window package. To keep the performance image pure, a 'Cuda could not be ordered with a slant six engine. The smallest V8 was the 318 LA engine which went unchanged from 1970, and was the base V8 for the Barracuda and Gran Coupe, optional on the Coupe package. It was now rated at 155hp at 4400rpm.

The demise of the AAR 'Cuda, along with its engine, meant there was only one other LA based engine, the 340 4-barrel – but what an engine! This smallblock mill offered the best power to weight ratio fitted in any E-body. Equipped with a Carter Thermo-Quad 4-barrel carburettor and a large unsilenced pancake air cleaner with no snorkel, this dream of an engine gave out 235hp (net) at 5000rpm, more than enough to power the big E-body cars from 0 to 60mph in just 6.4 seconds.

The big B-block 383 engine was now down to two versions, with the lowest powered 4-barrel being dropped to leave the 2-barrel, 190hp (net) mill and the high-performance 250hp (net) Super Commando 383. The first of these was painted blue and fitted with a 2-barrel Rochester GV carb topped by a crackle-paint pancake air-cleaner. Exhaust gases exited via a singular exhaust system. The Super Commando was the standard fitment in the 'Cuda, and for the most part was again painted Hemi Orange, although it is known that some 383s were painted blue. It was topped by a single Holley 4160 4-barrel carb with an unsilenced dual snorkel air cleaner, although most buyers went for the Shaker hood option. This larger 383 received a 1 point drop in compression, down to 8.5:1, allowing the use of regular gas. Only available in the 'Cuda (and Challenger R/T), the 440 returned but the lower-powered Super Commando was gone. The remaining 6-barrel option went virtually unchanged except for a reduction in compression ratio to 10.3:1, giving a power rating of 330 (net) at 4700rpm. It still used three Holley 2300 2-barrel carburettors

1971 RTS First there was the car ... next evolved the 'Supercar' ... then came THE SYSTEM. The Rapid Transit System returned again in 1971, along with the Dodge Scat Pack.

topped by the same oval, open-element filter held in position with a Hemi Orange metal cover.

This was the final year for the elephantine 426 Hemi, and like the 440, it had no obvious changes. Due to the lack of Hemi sales, over-production saw some of these engines date back to 1969. They still utilised the Carter 4742S carburettor at the front, and either the 4745S or 4746S at the rear, depending on transmission choice. Painted Hemi Orange, of course, except for the black crackle-finish valve covers, it came with a Shaker hood as standard. The 426 and the 440 had a reduced warranty of just 12 months/12,000 miles, and due to California's new drive-by noise regulations, neither the 426 nor 440 engines could be fitted with unsilenced air filters in that state. More muffled intakes were fitted when delivered to California.

With the base price for a 'Cuda hardtop coming in at $3155, and the 340 V8 being so capable, it is easy to see why only 129 buyers paid the extra $884 needed for the Hemi. Only 11 of these were built as convertibles, 7 of which were made for the US domestic market, 2 for Europe, and 2 for Canada. This makes the 1971 Hemi 'Cuda the rarest Hemi-powered car around, and the ultimate pony car – a fact reflected in some of the prices recently paid at auction. In 2005, one of the Hemi 'Cuda convertibles built for Europe sold in the USA for $4.1 million, breaking all records for a seventies muscle car. Another sold in 2007 for $3 million. On the very rare occasions that these cars come up for sale, only buyers with the deepest pockets bid.

Each double page of the RTS brochure focused on one of the different lines. This is how the pages for the 'Cuda looked.

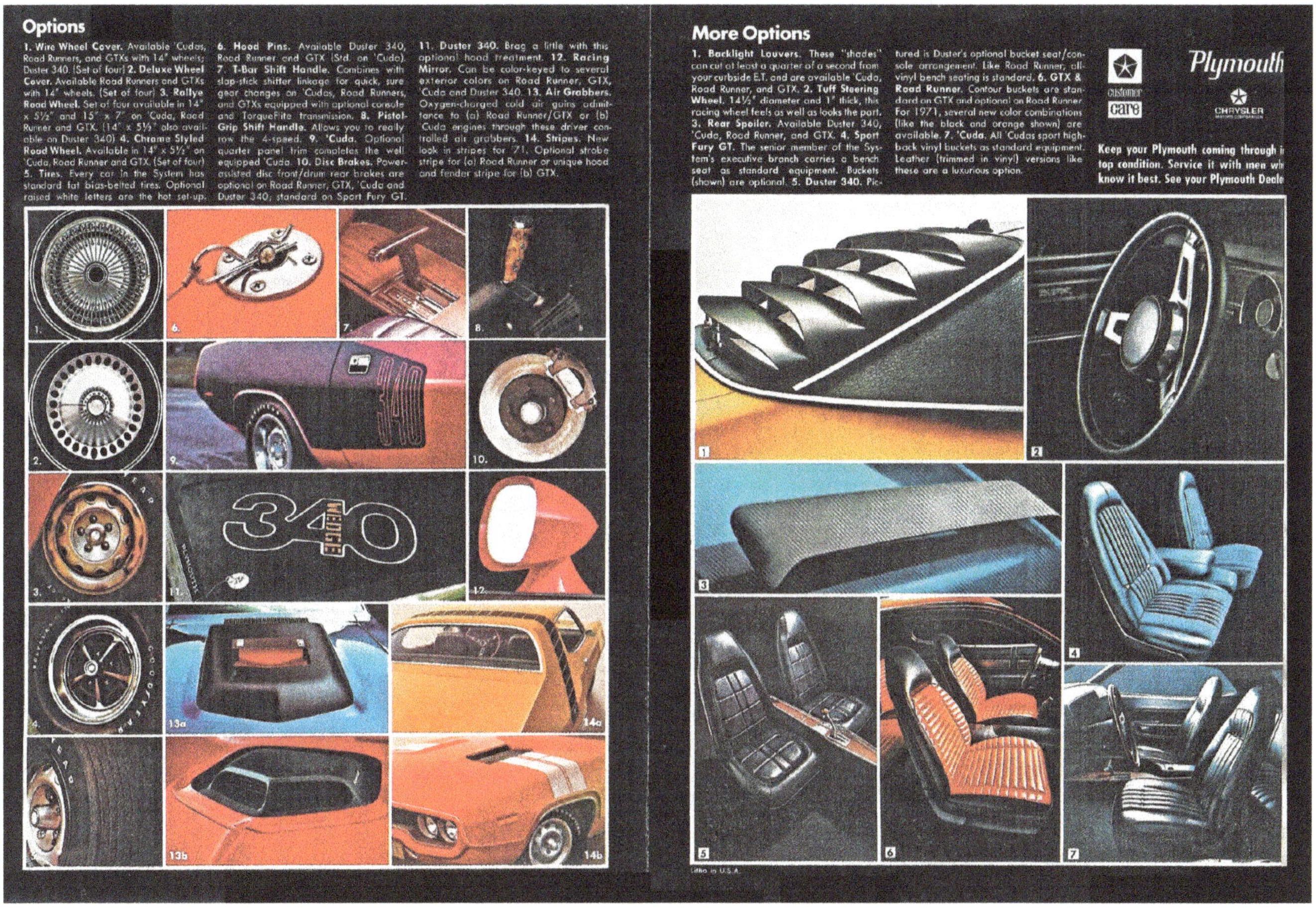

The ultimate pony car – 1971

Near the back of the RTS brochure were the options pages with a long list of must-have kit to bolt on to your Mopar, including wheels, tires, spoilers and backlight louvers.

Steve Kelly of *Hot Rod* magazine wrote in the January 1971 issue that the 'Cuda 340 was still the best catch. "The 'Cuda 340 is the kind of car a person could like, it runs low-14 without breathing hard, takes corners without yelling and is big enough to be seen." He admitted that the 340 was not the best Trans-Am car but went on to suggest that it was better than the Camaro Z28 or Mustang Boss 302.

The legend of the 1971 Barracuda was helped in 1996 when *Miami Vice* star Don Johnson was asked what kind of car he wanted to drive in his new TV series *Nash Bridges*. Johnson had seen a yellow 1971 Hemi 'Cuda convertible in a book and was adamant that was the car he was going to use; an American car for an American cop hero. When the

Don Grotheer was still a major force in drag racing, and can be seen here lifting the front wheels of his new 1971 Plymouth 'Cuda. (Courtesy Chrysler Historical Collection)

Dodge Challenger & Plymouth Barracuda

The legend of the 1971 Barracuda was helped in 1996 when Miami Vice *star Don Johnson was asked what kind of car he wanted to drive in his new TV series* Nash Bridges. *He chose the 1971 Hemi 'Cuda, although because of their rarity, none of the cars in the show were actually fitted with a Hemi engine. The cop show ran for six seasons on CBS from 29 March 1996 to 4 May 2001; a total of 122 episodes were produced, with the car becoming as big a part of the story as the actors.*

production company found out how rare the car was, and how in all likelihood it would get trashed during filming, they compromised and bought four Barracuda convertibles, two 1970 and two 1971 cars, and cloned them to look like the Hemi 'Cuda Johnson had seen. Oddly, none were fitted with a Hemi engine for the program, but all were given a black Shaker hood, white upholstery, white convertible top, Elastomeric front bumper, factory Rallye wheels and a pair of painted racing mirrors. The paint caused some problems because the car the actor had seen was finished in high-impact Lemon Twist, but this was found to be too bright for filming, so a School Bus Yellow was substituted.

The cop show ran for six seasons on CBS from 29 March 1996 to 4 May 2001, a total of 122 episodes being produced, with the car becoming as big a part of the story as the actors. The popularity of the show, and the car in particular, was reflected when one of the Nash Bridges clone cars came up for auction in 2003, going for many times over its actual worth and beating prices paid for real 'Cuda convertibles.

This was not the only time that a 'Cuda had made it big time and featured in a TV series. Mannix was an American television detective series that ran from 1967 through to 1975 on CBS. The series was created by Richard Levinson and William Link and developed by executive producer Bruce Geller. From series four, the title character, Joe Mannix, an Armenian-American private investigator played by Mike Connors, got rid of his Dodge Dart and drove a 1970 'Cuda ragtop fitted with a 340. The following year saw him update to a 1971 version of the same model, and then again in the next series he was seen driving a 1972 'Cuda 340 convertible.

But hang on, Plymouth didn't make a convertible in 1972 ... or did it?

Well, sadly, no. Joe Mannix's dark green metallic (EF8) model was the same 1971 car updated to look like a 1972 'Cuda with parts supplied by Plymouth. The tough, Dean Martin lookalike, renowned for being shot at and knocked unconscious, used this car through the sixth '72-73 season before moving to an Autumn Bronze Dodge Challenger for season seven, and ending up with a Camaro before the series was dropped.

Overall sales for the Barracuda were poor, with only 18,690 units built, down more than 36,000 units from the previous year's total of 55,499. One could hardly describe the Barracuda as innovative in its specification, and it gained very low sales because of that, but it still became the quintessential muscle car: handsome and brazen in its styling and filled to the brim with iconic features and gimmicks, none more so iconic than those cars with the big V8 engines under their hoods: 340, 340 Six Pak, 383 Magnum, 440 Magnum, 440 Six Pak, and of course, the legendary 426 Hemi. This would be the last year for the so-called Elephant engine, and the last year for Dodge and Plymouth convertibles for that matter.

1971 Challenger

For 1971, the Dodge Challenger maintained its basic body form from the previous year. Available in two series, the base Challenger and performance R/T models, the Challenger T/A was initially advertised but never produced, as Dodge had withdrawn from Trans Am racing. The most basic Challenger was still the A93 coupe package using the body code JH23 hardtop coupe. The other base Challengers

The 1971 Challenger came in two series: the base Challenger seen here in this press release photo, and the Challenger R/T. They received a new rear light setup to match the new front grille, consisting of two thinner bezels and the Challenger script held in the centre below the trunk lock.

There is absolutely no doubt that these cars were beautiful, but everything was against them being successful. Larger and more expensive than its Ford rival, Dodge had arrived much too late in the diminishing pony and muscle car markets. Sales dropped dramatically in 1971, down to 29,883 from the previous year's total of 83,032.

DODGE NEWS PHOTO

COMPACT SPORTS -- The 1971 Dodge Challenger is a sporty compact with more interior room and a low price tag. Three models: coupe, hardtop and convertible. Choice of 10 engines, many accessories including Cassette stereo and air conditioning.

From: Dodge Public Relations, P.O. Box 1259, Detroit, Michigan 48231
For Release On or After Sunday, September 6, 1970   (71-2307-RP)

The R/T carried the same new grille, although the designer for this, Jeff Godshall, planned to have two snorkels on each side of the divide of the R/T to distinguish it from the base model. His proposal was turned down because of cost. The hood now carried large cutout R/T decals on the front centre.

were the JH23 hardtop and JH27 convertible, the only convertible left in the entire Dodge range. All base Challengers (except the Deputy package) came with a 225in^3 slant six or 318in^3 V8, cigarette lighter, ashtray, color-coded carpeting, front and rear side arm rests, heater and defroster, dual horns, dome light, parking brake warning light, left door mirror, interior day/night mirror, bucket seats, simulated woodgrain three-spoke steering wheel, electric windshield washer and two-speed wipers. The convertible also had front courtesy and pocket panel lights, along with a space saver spare tire in the trunk.

The R/T was now, sadly, only available as a hardtop and could not be had as a convertible or with the SE trim. The R/Ts came with everything fitted to the base Challenger, along with a 383in^3 V8 as standard, heavy-duty brakes and Rallye suspension, woodgrain Rallye instrument cluster, chrome exhaust tips, variable speed windscreen wipers, dummy air intakes on the rear flanks, and unique R/T body stripes.

Jeff Godshall was a designer working in the Dodge studio at that time. Arriving in the early sixties, he finally retired from Chrysler as an executive in late 2008. It was his talent that created the

The ultimate pony car – 1971

The Challenger convertible was the only soft-top left in the whole of the Dodge range, and this, too, would be gone the following year. This Plum Crazy example is fitted with the powerful 440 Six Pak performance option topped with a Shaker hood. It carries the correct twin R/T bodyside stripes that finish where the C-pillar would come down.

facelift for the 1971 Challenger. Main changes for all Challengers included a revised front grille and a modified rear end. The grille now featured two, thinner openings that extended across the whole of the grille to where the quad headlamps resided. Slightly canted outwards as they met in the centre, the bezels were painted silver, contrasting with the black surround. The lower valance and air intake remained unchanged from the previous year.

I spoke with Jeff recently, and he told me: "With regard to the '71 Challenger, I was responsible for the new twin-snorkel grille and similar-appearing taillights. Originally, the R/T was to have a four-snorkel grille, two to the left of centerline, two to the right, but the product planners nixed the idea of a unique R/T grille due to cost. I had three E-bodies. My first was a '70 'Cuda with the 340 CID V8 and a 4-speed transmission. I then had a '71 Challenger R/T with a 383 V8, and finally, a '72 'Cuda 340. The latter two had Torqueflite automatics. My cars were equipped with Rim Blow steering wheels in which a small black rubber membrane on the inside of the wheel trim served as the horn. Just a light squeeze and the horn blew. No need to lift your hand off the wheel to sound the horn. Trouble was the system was not 'robust,' and was therefore subject to numerous warranty repairs."

At the back of the car, the taillights had also shrunk and complemented the front with two thinner bezels and the Challenger script held in the centre below the trunk lock. The exhausts exited from the same cutouts situated at the bottom of the lower valance. The spoiler package could still be ordered but the rear 'Go-wing' lost its downward-sloping ends and became flatter.

Along with set packages like the coupe and Formal Roof Package (A78) that replaced the SE, a host of options were on offer. Vinyl and leather or cloth and vinyl buckets seats, woodgrain finish centre console, a Formal Roof package (A78) that replaced the SE (which was not available to R/Ts anymore), a floor-mounted radio-cassette tape player with recorder, vinyl roof, backlight louver pack, and sliding sunroof to name but a few. At $445.85, the powered sliding sunroof was not a

There was only one version of the 440 on the options list in 1971, and that was the 440 Six Pak (called a 440 Six Barrel in the Plymouth). The compression ratio was lowered to 10.3:1 to give a rating of 330 horsepower (net) at 3200rpm. The three twin Holley carbs were usually topped by an orange-painted, oval open-element air cleaner, but could be had with the Shaker fresh air intake. The battery is not original.

If you got the Shaker intake and special hood, you got the sticker to go with it!

cheap option and found few buyers. It came with a vinyl roof, lining, and operating switch set in the roof inclusive in the price. Elastomeric body-color bumpers were new for the Challenger in 1971 and came in four hues: Bright Blue Metallic, Hemi Orange, Citron Yella and Plum Crazy. Part way through the year, most of the colors were dropped except Citron Yella. Engines and paint schemes reflected

The side view shows how low and sexy the Challenger was. The 1971 cars grew two fake gills on each rear flank. This car carries the correct R/T side stripes and road wheels, but sensibly the crossply tires have been replaced by radials.

exactly what was on offer in the Barracuda and 'Cuda series.

The year 1971 saw a change in hoods and decals too. The base Challenger fitted with a slant six, 318 or 2-barrel 383 had a flat steel hood similar to that used on the '70 but had a new front trim molding. The Dodge Tri-star badge sat in the same front central position. All larger engined cars came with the steel R/T hood, which featured a domed centre that held two simulated air intakes. This hood could have the raised section finished in black (on the R/T) or body-color, and carried no badges, although engine identification could be placed on the raised sides. The exception to this was when the R/T hood was fitted to an R/T model; this would

The 1971 Challengers came with a chrome, manually-controlled mirror mounted on the driver's door. Optional was a chrome or body-colored, remote-controlled 'racing' mirror. A matching right side 'racing' mirror was available, but this was not remote-controlled.

Dodge Challenger & Plymouth Barracuda

The interior of the 1971 Challenger went virtually unchanged from the previous year. This convertible has the performance Rallye dash that holds a tachometer, electric clock and 150mph speedometer. A fourth pod holds fuel, water temperature, amps and oil pressure gauge. Going from top left clockwise, the small knobs on the left are: headlamps, wiper/washers, power top and panel dimmer switch. Below these is a switch for the rear speakers. The car also has the Rim Blow steering wheel, Hurst pistol grip for the performance 4-speed manual gearbox, and pedal dress-up kit.

carry large R/T outline decals front and centre in black. The Shaker hood was still popular on larger engined cars and came with hood tie-down pins, but could not be had with air conditioning. Decals now consisted of two horizontal stripes that ran along three quarters of the car, accentuating the

The ultimate pony car – 1971

1971 Scat Pack. By 1971 membership dues had risen to $5.95, but it was still one hell of a bargain. This is the front cover for that year's Scat Pack brochure, featuring the Charger and Demon.

character line. Standard on the R/T and optional on other models, they started at the tip of the front fender and finished under the rear quarter light. When fitted to an R/T the stripes finished with an R/T callout.

To most, there is absolutely no doubt that these cars were beautiful, but everything was against them being successful. Dodge had arrived much too late in the diminishing pony and muscle car markets. Sales dropped dramatically in 1971 down to 29,883 from the previous year's total of 83,032. In a bid to help, a small group of local Dodge dealers (Capitol Dodge, McGinty Dodge, Palmer Dodge, and Shadeland Dodge) tried to boost Challenger sales by providing fifty specially prepared examples of the official pace cars for the Indianapolis 500 race. They were shown at the race with a handful being used by officials, and then sold on to the public, available with or without the side lettering. Challengers were the only convertible in the whole Dodge range, and it was one of these fifty convertibles that was to pace the 55th Indy 500. All fifty cars were painted EV2 Hemi Orange and had white interiors and a white roof, although only two had high-performance options. Because of the high speeds involved in the task, the actual pace car had a 383 Magnum (4-barrel) motor, as did the backup car, while three others had 383 2-barrel mills. Three more were fitted with the 340 engine while the rest were fitted with 318s.

Although it was an attractive pace car it has generally been forgotten, which is just how Dodge would like it kept, because it was this pace car that lost control while trying to exit the track and hit a group of journalists, seriously injuring over twenty of them. On race day (29 May 1971) the pace car was driven by one of the local dealers called Eldon Palmer of Palmer Dodge, Indianapolis. In the car with Palmer on race day were Speedway owner Tony Hulman, television sportscaster Chris Schenkel and astronaut John Glenn.

Palmer had quite rightly practised going around the circuit and had a flag placed at a strategic point to indicate when to start to turn in and when to brake. On race day, however, somebody moved the flag, and as he came out of turn four with the 33-car field hot on his tail, he dived down into the pit area as planned and started looking for his marker. By the time he realised it was missing it was too late. As he slammed on the brakes he saw he had two options: either go back out onto the track and hit the pack of accelerating race cars or just keep braking as best he could in a straight line. He did the latter but lost control and failed to stop in time to miss the stand full of press photographers. There was much speculation at the time that if the car had been fitted with optional disc brakes instead of the standard drum brakes this tragedy might have been avoided. But these cars were not supplied by Dodge, they were bought privately by the four dealers, which is why they were not fully loaded and had standard issue brakes, hoods, etc.

1971 Challenger T/A. Although Dodge advertised the 1971 T/A within an eight page advert for the Scat Pack published in Hot Rod magazine in October 1970, it was never built. The image used was the same one featured in 1970, but with a 1971 grille superimposed. Chrysler's decision to cease competing in the SCCA's Trans-Am series at the end of 1970 put paid to any hope of a production model.

Traditionally, the winner of the race, in this case Al Unser, would have won the pace car along with his prize money, but Palmer kept the car and after some time, had it repaired. Not surprisingly, after this incident the pace car decal sets available through Dodge dealers did not sell well.

As expected, sales dropped for 1971, making the Challengers and Barracudas from this year even more sought-after today. The Hemi-powered Challenger coupes and ultra-rare Barracuda convertibles can be priced in their millions, but back then salesmen had a very hard time trying to sell these cars. It wasn't just the E-bodies though; the late sixties and early seventies were a bad time for Chrysler particularly, and not just because of the economic and social environment. As well as poor judgement on what the public wanted, Chrysler cars had been suffering from poor fit and finish, along with problems caused by the company's new computer system. Cars were arriving at the wrong locations with the wrong accessories installed. The future wasn't looking rosy for employees of the Chrysler Corporation.

It ain't Attila the Hun, but it ain't Mary Mild either. Standard engine was the 383 on the R/T, but buyers could still choose a 340, 440 or 426 Hemi from the options list.

Dodge Challenger Pace Car. Dodge was selected to pace the Indy 500 race in 1971, and as it only had one convertible in production – the Challenger – that was the car used. Two cars were supplied to the race course by local Dodge dealers for use as pacers, while another fifty convertibles were painted in the same Hemi Orange with white soft-top and matching interior for sale afterwards, with optional pace car decals. At the end of the pace lap, driver Eldon Palmer of Palmer Dodge lost control and ploughed into a press stand, injuring many of the photographers. This ignominious incident was the only accident to happen in the history of the Indy 500 that would involve a pace car. After the crash, the car was not given to the winner as was the ritual, but was retrieved by Palmer and eventually repaired.

The 1971 Diamante was the result of combining two production vehicles, the Challenger and Charger, and was penned by Bob Ackerman. A clay model was done of this car using the Ackerman design on the front and a pre-production cast of the '72 taillights in the rear. A sculptured, sloping front end added downward air pressure and included aerodynamic retractable headlamps. Side-mounted exhaust pipes and air intakes ventilated and cooled the 426in^3 Hemi V8 that powered the rear wheels via a 4-speed manual transmission. Inside the bright orange-colored car, a removable roof panel revealed a built in chrome roll-bar. The rear windscreen, housed in the flying buttress roof panel, could be electrically lowered from the driver's position. Milt Antonick followed the development of this car from clay model to fully-engineered vehicle at a local fabrication shop. It was originally painted 3-coat pearlescent white and was later changed to a pearl orange, although the current owner has returned it to its original look. If you think it looks familiar, that's because this car was the Yellow Jacket from 1970 until it was modified and renamed! (Courtesy Steven Juliano)

5

SCALING DOWN – 1972-1974

Every pony car in the market took a big hit in sales for 1972, but if there was any doubt that the end of the muscle car era had arrived, one only had to look at what was on offer from Dodge and Plymouth to see that they had given up on the horsepower war. In the case of the Barracuda, this once muscular car was reverting to a pony car – a less powerful, yet highly driveable sports car. But it was a season of cut backs. The decision to drop the Challenger and Barracuda had already been made; it was just a matter of squeezing out a few more dollars in sales from the doomed E-bodies by reducing production costs.

The series was reduced to offer just two models: the base JH23 Challenger and JS23 Rallye for Dodge, and the matching BH23 Barracuda and BS23 'Cuda for Plymouth, all of which were based on the same hardtop body. The coupes and convertibles were consigned to the history books. The vast array of engines withered down to just three choices: the 225 slant six and 318 for the base Barracuda and Challenger, and the 318 and a detuned 340 V8 for the 'Cuda and R/T replacement, the Rallye. The options list grew shorter, and even the advertising was depressing – the ad for the '72 Challenger Rallye read: "The way things are today, maybe what you need is not the world's hottest car. Maybe what you need is a well-balanced, fully instrumented road machine. One with a highly individualized style, a well proportioned balance between acceleration, road holding, braking – you

A clay model of the planned 1972 Challenger, right? Wrong! This photo, taken in the Plymouth studio in 1969, shows a proposal by stylist Dick Watson for the front end of the 1972 Barracuda. It is not clear whose design came first, Watson's or Bob Ackerman's in the Dodge studio, but the Plymouth design had to be dropped as it was nearly identical to the Challenger. Ackerman told me about the 'sad face' grille: "I had no idea that the Plymouth studio was even pursuing this design direction. It must have been Dick who had the 'sad face.' Dodge general manager Bob McCurry and styling director Bill Brownlie picked my sketch as the final theme for the Challenger." A design by Don Hood was used on the Plymouth instead, along with his fender vents. Shortly after this, the studios were reorganized into body lines, not divisions, removing the competitiveness and some of the problems of repetition.

Another clay model for the 1972 Barracuda. The grille detail has yet to be finished while the hood is being done separately. Note that the decision whether to fit two or four headlamps has yet to be taken. In the background is one of the ill-fated designs for the next generation of E-bodies.

Robert (Bob) Ackerman grew up in Waterbury, CT, and enrolled at the Art Center School in Los Angeles in 1956. After just one year he had run out of funds and had to leave. He then found a job at Rockwell Aviation working on the X-15 project, and in 1960 moved to General Motors. In 1964 Bob won a design contest sponsored by Motor Trend *magazine and received a full scholarship to the Art Center. After finishing his studies, Ackerman returned to GM, working in the Oldsmobile and Chevrolet studios. In 1969 he moved to Chrysler and worked on the Dodge Challenger. Bob stayed with Chrysler for the remainder of his career, retiring in 1996. This is one of his ideas for the 1972 Challenger, executed in Prismacolor markers, a popular medium at that time in the studios. (Courtesy Brett Snyder)*

know the bit." In fact, everything a pony car used to be, and a far cry from the virtues being extolled just two years before.

With the loss of Dodge's Charger R/T and Super Bee and Plymouth's GTX, both the Rapid Transit System and Dodge's Scat Pack were gone; performance was an ugly word, and not just for the Mopar guys. Production of the Camaro had dived from its sales of 243,095 in 1969 to just 68,656 by 1972, and the Mustang had faired little better. The big Boss fastbacks had been dropped and sales peaked at 125,093. Although this figure looks high, in 1969 just one model alone, the Mustang hardtop coupe, sold more than that.

151

Initially, the stylists were working on a completely new front end for the 1972 E-bodies, but further cutbacks reduced this to minor facelifts of the front and rear. The accompanying sketches by Bob Ackerman show the phase of the program when they were working on the all-new front end, from the firewall forward. (Courtesy Robert Ackerman)

SCALING DOWN – 1972-1974

Scaling down – 1972-1974

Also by Ackerman, this shows the finished front end sketch that went on the car, minus the final grille texture proposal, which was done with quick thumbnail sketches and working directly on the clay model. (Courtesy Robert Ackerman)

The 'Cuda was now in the background as this Plymouth brochure shows. Emphasis had definitely fallen away from the performance side and turned back to where it all started for the pony car, as a driveable sports car with great handling and power to get you to your destination.

1972 Barracuda

The E-body Barracuda and 'Cuda received their third and final alteration in front end styling this year. Milt Antonick told me about the last big change: "Studios were reorganized based on vehicle type instead of brands or car lines. I briefly had both Barracuda as well as Challenger so I was responsible for the last Challenger design, as well as the Barracuda. I believe Bob Ackerman did the theme sketch." Indeed, Bob Ackerman did design the last facelift for the Challenger, along with the Diamante show car.

For the Plymouth, the busy grille from '71 reverted to a handsome, simpler design, very reminiscent of the 1970 models. It featured a large central divider painted Argent Silver that held three

Dodge Challenger & Plymouth Barracuda

The facelift was done by talented stylist Milt Antonick. The front grille harked back to the 1970 series Barracuda, but had a wider central divide, painted Argent Silver, that held three deep vertical slots on each side. On each side of the centre piece were deeply-recessed black grilles with horizontal bars and four vertical dividers. The round headlamps were again reduced to two, and were held in squared-off, chrome-finish housings. The performance hood went unchanged but was available with a neat paint job. It could be finished in black, except for the area leading up to and including the simulated hood scoops, which remained body-color, transforming the look of the front end.

Scaling down – 1972-1974

deep vertical slots on each side. On each side of the centre piece were deeply recessed black grilles with horizontal bars and four vertical dividers. The round headlamps were again reduced to two and were held in squared-off, chrome-finish housings. The chrome gills on the front fenders did not reappear for 1972, but Barracuda name badges were placed on the doors near the A-pillar just above the character line.

The rear valance also received its most dramatic change this year; the taillights were now housed in four round pods with the reversing lights placed inside the inner lights, as made popular by the Camaro. The panel itself was painted black on the 'Cuda with stainless steel trim, and the Barracuda and 'Cuda nameplate moved from the right of the licence plate to the left. Decals were simplified with black body stripes, optional at $29.40 or standard if the buyer picked the Sport Décor Group trim package, although an interesting hood treatment was optional on the 'Cuda. The performance hood could be finished in black except for the area leading up to, and including, the simulated hood scoops, which remained body-color.

Color choice was trimmed down slightly, too, with body-colors now available in only thirteen standard and two high-impact colors. Base colors were Blue Sky HB1, Rallye Red FE5, Amber Sherwood Metallic GF3, Spinnaker White EW1, Formal Black TX9, Honeydew GY4, Gold Leaf Metallic GY8, Tawny Gold Metallic GY9, Chestnut Metallic HT8, Winchester Gray Metallic GA4, Mojave Tan Metallic HT6, Basin Street Blue TB3 and True Blue Metallic GB5. The two extra cost paints were Tor-Red EV2 and Lemon Twist FY1. These colors could be complemented with a choice of three vinyl roof colors (Black, White and Green), five interiors of Bright Blue, Dark Green, White, Black or Gold, and a choice of six colored or chrome racing mirrors.

The base Barracuda had a shorter list of standard equipment, including a 225 six or 318 V8 engine, dual horns, hub caps, painted 14in steel wheels, interior day/night mirror, brake warning light, left wing mirror, bucket seats, cigarette lighter, color-coded nylon loop-pile carpet, and 7.35 x 14 Goodyear black sidewall tires. Additionally, the 'Cuda received stainless steel wheel lip and sill moldings, performance hood, heavy-duty

Dodge Challenger & Plymouth Barracuda

The coupes and convertibles were consigned to the history books. The vast array of engines withered down to just three choices; the 225 slant six and 318 for the base Barracuda and Challenger, and the 318 and a detuned 340 V8 for the 'Cuda and R/T replacement, the Rallye. This 1972 Barracuda has been set up for the strip although it is still road legal. It has a full roll-cage and the original engine has been swapped for a 383 Magnum. The billboard decal is incorrect for the year, but is so popular that many owners buy them for their E-body cars, regardless of the year – and why not?

The emphasis had changed. The ad for this 1972 Challenger Rallye reads "The way things are today, maybe what you need is not the world's hottest car. Maybe what you need is a well balanced, fully instrumented road machine. One with a highly individualized style, a well proportioned balance between acceleration, road holding, braking – you know the bit. This is it. The Challenger Rallye."

suspension, electronic ignition, wider F70 x 14 bias belted tires with whitewall sides, blacked-out rear valance and color-coded grille. All Barracudas (and Challengers) shared the same new two-spoke steering wheel that had a textured Coachman grain black polypropylene grip and bright steel spokes. The rest of the interior saw little change, although the optional centre console got a make-over.

With a decrease in standard equipment, the options list was still quite comprehensive and included air conditioning, radios, bumper guards, deluxe wheel covers, electric clock, a 4-speed manual transmission, interior hood release, Light package, right side wing mirror, left hand remote wing mirror, power front discs, power steering, Rallye road wheels, rear window defogger, sport décor package (Barracuda only), sun roof, Sure Grip differential, tinted glass, Torqueflite automatic gearbox, variable speed wipers and a vinyl roof.

Scaling down – 1972-1974

Because all of the most powerful engines had been dropped, so was the need for the Shaker hood, 15in wheels, the rugged Dana 60 rear axle and the choice of ratios that went with it. Savings were also made because only one type of front fender was necessary, and although they looked the same, there were new pressings. Standard transmission was the floor-mounted 3-speed manual gearbox mated to the 225in^3 slant six or 2-barrel 318 with a single exhaust pipe. The 4-speed manual was still an option but had to be matched to the 240hp (net) 340in^3 V8, and the Torqueflite automatic could be had with any of the three engines offered.

The Hurst pistol grip and Sure Grip differentials were also still available, and power brakes were now only supplied if front disc brakes were specified. A Hemi engine was available for purchase by racers for 'time trial purposes' only, but it is very likely that rules were bent so that some of these crate Hemis wound up under the hood of late E-bodies. Sales continued their downward trend with only 10,622 Barracudas and 7828 'Cudas finding homes that year. Sales brochures specific to the Barracuda were thin affairs, while Plymouth range brochures failed to have an image of the E-body on the cover, although the cars were listed inside. Emphasis was now being placed on the more affordable and insurable Duster and Valiant.

1972 Challenger

Matching the Barracuda lines, the Challenger for 1972 was down to just two models, the base Challenger and Challenger Rallye, both of which underwent little change. The facelift consisted

The front of the Challenger took on a sad-faced look for '72, perhaps in frustration at its diminishing power. It would keep this styling until its demise in 1974. The mesh grille on the Rallye models was painted matt black while the base Challenger grilles were finished in Argent Silver.

Dodge Challenger & Plymouth Barracuda

1972 Challenger. Just two Challengers remained by 1972: the base model two-door hardtop that cost $2790, and the performance Rallye version that used the same body and took the price up to $3082. The Rallye replaced the R/T models and the convertible was gone. This 1972 Dodge Challenger Rallye came to the UK from California in 1990, and had a number of owners, including Virgin Records, which bought it to promote Mariah Carey's European tour.

of a new sad-faced front grille designed by Bob Ackerman, which featured a wide mesh grille finished in black that sat in a simple body-colored front panel, which also held the traditional quad headlamps. The Challenger script was placed on the right of the mesh grille. The script was also found on each rear fender above the character line and side marker. Also penned by Ackerman was the new lower valance that held a smaller air intake and round side/indicator lights.

Ackerman remembers: "When I arrived in August 1969 from General Motors, I first saw the all new '73-'74 Challenger Barracuda proposals. They were quite advanced, but unfortunately because of corporate financial difficulties, they were scheduled to be cancelled. Rising fuel costs and new federal legislation was signalling the end of the muscle car era. The program was then reduced to changing the car from the cowl forward and new taillamps, which is what I was involved with. Later, the program was thrifted again to head lamps, grille insert, valance panel and taillight panels.

"The '72 clay model was accomplished by two very talented clay sculptors. On the front was Jim Romeo, on the rear was Rick Zaleski. Many proposals were tried and what ended up being the '72 front end was deemed the most change for the money. The grille texture was worked out on the clay model with only thumbnail sketches and designer direction."

The rear taillamp panel held two large lamps on either side, angled towards each other and mounted on a plain panel, painted black Organosol on the Rallye and medium Astrotone on the base model. Black 'Dodge' lettering was centred between the light pods just below the trunk lock. The bumper was

Scaling down – 1972-1974

1972 Challenger. The Barracuda/Challenger door trim panels were the first instance of having a door trim panel composed entirely of injection-molded plastic. It was a good idea and ahead of the times, but the door panels rattled terribly in service and caused a drum-like boom instead of the more traditional clunk when the door closed. They went almost unchanged from 1970 through to the E-body's demise in 1974.

the same one fitted in late 1971. New simulated air extractors on each fender were standard on the Rallye, and came with neat black strobe effect decals stretching out to almost the entire length of the door.

Base Challengers could be had with an optional bodyside protection stripe, but in recent years many owners have chosen to fit the twin stripes from 1971. The side markers were rationalised with the Barracuda and were cheaper-looking plastic rectangles. The pop-up sports filler cap remained high on the left flank and was available with the Rallye package, while the body-color twist cap was standard.

Only two hoods were available for this year: the base flat steel hood and the performance hood, also pressed from steel. This power bulge hood with simulated air intakes was similar to the previous year's design, and came standard on the Rallye and optional on a base Challenger when ordered with the 340 V8. As well as the performance hood and fake air intakes on the front fenders, the Rallye came with stainless-tipped exhaust, dual horns, racing mirror and simulated woodgrain Rallye dash. The colored urethane Elastomeric bumpers were not available on the Challenger or Barracuda/'Cuda.

Paint choices almost matched those available for the Barracuda with a few name changes along the way, and included standard colors Light Blue HB1, Bright Blue Metallic HB5, Bright Red FE5, Light Green Metallic GF3, Dark Green Metalic GF7, Eggshell White GW1, Black TX9, Light Gold GY5, Gold Metallic GY8, Dark Gold Metallic GY9, Dark Tan Metallic GT8, Light Gunmetal Metallic GA4, Medium Tan Metallic GA4 and Super Blue GB3. High-impact colors were Hemi Orange EV2 and Top Banana FY1. The Challenger interior saw few detail changes. Trim was available in five colors – black, white, blue, green and gold – and could only be had in vinyl as the cloth and leather options had been deleted.

Challengers had some of the largest doors in the industry, and as in previous years, the door panel was made up of one large ABS plastic panel molded in one of the interior trim colors. 1972 saw a mild change to the molding, with the door handles being recessed and arm rests integrated in the panel. The optional central console (option C16) also underwent a mild redesign, but kept its asymmetrical style. It came in two different moldings and was used with manual and automatic cars, although at a glance they looked the same.

Other options matched those offered on the Plymouths, including a Light package (A01) that came with ashtray lamp, trunk lamp, glove box lamp, map/courtesy lamp, ignition switch lamp with time delay, time-delay instrument panel

This well optioned, matching-numbers Rallye has a vinyl roof, sports fuel filler cap, correct Rallye road wheels, and is finished in FY1 Top Banana. When it was built on the second assembly line at Hamtramck on 30 August 1972, it also had the fender-mounted turn signals, but these were removed at some point.

The famous sports fuel filler cap, introduced on the early Barracudas and borrowed by Dodge for its Chargers and Challengers. This was optional on all Challenger models, although standard with some packages.

floodlight, fender mounted turn signals, buzzer, and a 'headlight on' reminder. The Basic Group package (A04) consisted of an AM radio (various upgrades could be ordered at extra cost), power steering, left remote mirror, variable speed wipers and electric washers. Power sunroof (M51), body sill moldings (M25), rear window defroster (H31), and air conditioning (H51) could also be ticked off on the options sheet. The SE package was not available, so neither was the more formal roof with smaller back

Because of federal regulations for bumpers to absorb an impact at 5mph, Challenger and Barracuda bumpers were strengthened and moved forward, causing a gap between the bumper and bodywork, so a rubberised silver painted filler was used to pack the space. This was introduced on late-'72 cars and all E-bodies thereafter.

windscreen.

The vast array of engines available just twelve months before had dwindled down to three choices. Base powerplant was the 225in^3 slant six that produced 100hp (net) at 4000rpm and came with the same single-barrel Holley 1920 carburettor fitted in the first Challengers. This medium-blue painted engine breathed through a satin-black finished silenced air cleaner with wing nut fastener, and was only fitted to the base Challenger. It found 842 buyers.

The base V8 for the Challenger and Challenger Rallye was the same 318 as fitted in the Barracuda; with its 3.91 x 3.31 bore and stroke and compression ratio of 8.6:1 it offered a net horsepower rating of 150hp. This LA-based engine was painted Chrysler engine medium blue, and came with a Carter BBD two-barrel carb and a satin black-finish, pie-tin-style air cleaner.

The only other engine available in 1972 was another LA engine, the veritable jewel that was the 340. Admittedly it had a reduced compression ratio of 8.5:1 instead of 10.3:1, but it could now run on regular gas and still offered an impressive 240hp (net). Underneath the single snorkel Hemi Orange air cleaner sat a Carter Thermoquad 4-barrel carb. This engine came with dual exhausts and a floor mounted three-speed, fully synchronised manual gearbox, but extra performance could be had by ordering the 4-speed manual transmission and A36 hi-po axle package. This came with a 3.55:1 heavy-duty axle, Sure Grip diff, larger radiator, fan shroud,

1972 saw the introduction of a new two-spoke steering wheel shared with the Plymouth. This car has the Rallye instrument cluster and woodgrain-topped centre console. The console had a very mild makeover and was a new pressing for this year, but you would have to look hard to spot the differences between years. The car is fitted with the heavy-duty 4-speed manual transmission and Hurst wooden pistol grip changer.

The new fender louvers were strikingly different, and were accentuated by the strobo-effect black stripes leading from the fender to most of the way through the door. They were standard on the Rallye package, along with the performance hood and Rallye instrument cluster.

seven blade fan, and if fitted with power-steering, a power-steering oil cooler. Even without the extra performance axle pack, a 340-powered Challenger could do 0-60 in 8.5 seconds, and the quarter mile in 16 seconds.

Although Chrysler was giving its pony cars scant attention or publicity, a cheap way to gain

The rear of the car was created by Bob Ackerman and consisted of changes to the taillamp panel. It held two large lamps on each side, angled towards each other, mimicking the rectangular exhaust outlets below. As can be seen here, the lamps were mounted on a plain panel, painted black Organosol on the Rallye or medium Astrotone on the base model. Black 'Dodge' lettering was centred between the light pods just below the trunk lock. The bumper was the same one fitted in late 1971 with bumper guards.

maximum coverage was to sponsor a TV show by supplying the TV companies with vehicles. As Plymouth had done for *Mannix* with the 'Cuda, Dodge supplied a Challenger to CBS for use on the drama *Medical Center* that ran from 24 September 1969 to 6 September 1976. Based in a University Hospital in Los Angeles, Chad Everett played Doctor Joe Gannon, a young and rebellious surgeon who drove a 1972 Challenger convertible as his personal transportation for several seasons. As no convertibles were built by Dodge in 1972, they converted some

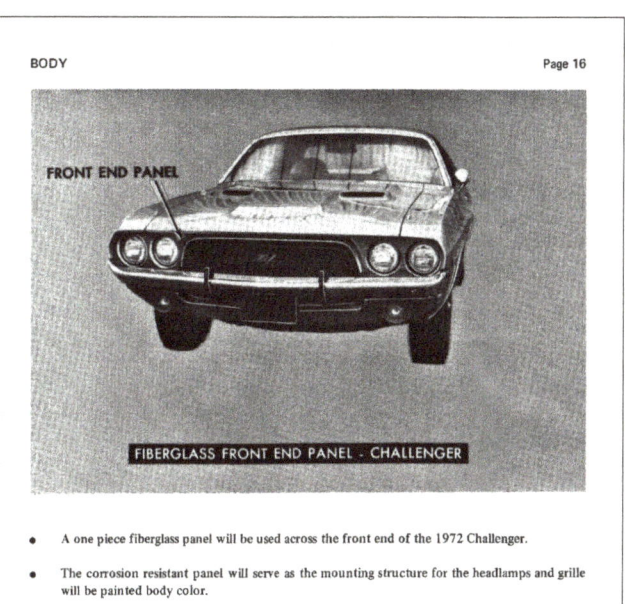

Although of poor quality, this is an important image. This page is in the 1972 Passenger car highlights booklet that was distributed to dealerships at the start of the model year as part of Chrysler's service training program for dealership service personnel. Although the image is dark, take note of the R/T emblem at the centre of the grille; it is not every day that you will see a picture of a 1972 R/T.

Dodge Challenger & Plymouth Barracuda

This Challenger is suffering from an identity crisis. It has had the bumper guards removed front and back, but a neat two-tone blue, non-original paint job applied. Over that are twin body-stripes reminiscent of the 1971 R/T side stripes, but longer. The paint does hide the fender louvers, unfortunately. The car also wears front and rear spoilers from a T/A and large chrome wheels with low profile tires. Passers-by at the Mopar EuroNationals in 2008 were positive about its looks; they either positively hated it, or positively loved it!

This Challenger is as black as it gets. The front panel is black to match the body-color paint; it also has the matt black finish on the optional performance hood, black strobe stripes coming from the fender louvers, and black vinyl interior. If the engine call-out is to be believed, this car has a 440 Six Pak fitted, which was not available after the 1971 model year. The chrome wheels are also incorrect.

Scaling down – 1972-1974

The rear is just as dark and is accentuated by the black light panel and Go-wing spoiler. The spoiler was not an option from the factory this year, but could be dealer-installed before delivery.

1971 models to look like 1972 cars, although it is not known how many Challengers received this treatment. As sales increased for the lighter Dart models, the Challenger sales continued their downward trend, if not quite as dramatically. There were 18,535 base Challengers and 8123 Challenger Rallyes built this year, making a grand total of 26,658 Challengers, just over 3200 down from 1971.

1973 Off the hook

1973 was another year of cutbacks for Chrysler's already emasculated E-bodies. Barracudas and Challengers were now being called personal sports compacts to further push them away from the muscle car image. Another engine, the 225in^3 slant six, fell by the wayside, a victim of Washington's stricter emissions regulations, but the cars themselves saw very little change. The Challenger Rallye was relegated to the position of an options package leaving just a base Challenger, although the 'Cuda remained a series in its own right. The A57 Rallye package consisted of a sport hood, fake air extractors and strobe decals on the fenders as fitted to the 1972 Challenger Rallye. It also came with heavy-duty suspension, sway bars, F70 x 14 tires, Rallye instrument cluster, chrome flip-up fuel filler cap and a matt black grille. The Rallye instrument cluster offered a 150mph speedometer, electric clock, 7000rpm tacho, oil pressure gauge and simulated woodgrain finish,

Dodge Challenger & Plymouth Barracuda

'Cuda & Barracuda

Sporty appearance and sporty performance. Barracuda and 'Cuda both come equipped with the 318 V-8 . . . a 340 V-8 is optional. Power front disc brakes, standard on the 'Cuda, Electronic Ignition System, bucket seats, unibody construction on both cars—plus a heavy-duty suspension system including front and rear sway bars and F70 x 14" white sidewall tires on 'Cuda. Dress-up options—sporty body side tape, Barracuda sports decor group, rallye wheels, chrome road wheels, vinyl roof, console.

SCALING DOWN – 1972-1974

Background: Barracuda Foreground: 'Cuda
Extra care in engineering... it makes a difference

There were no real styling changes for 1973, except for the addition of large ugly rubber-covered bumper guards front and back. As with the Challenger, the Barracuda and 'Cuda had a reinforced steel beam contoured to the back of the bumper for extra strength. The whole bumper was moved away from the body and the space filled with an Argent Silver plastic strip. The 6-cylinder engine was dropped this year, making the base engine the 318 V8, and the 340 an option. Electronic ignition was made standard on all engines. This image, taken from the Plymouth brochure for that year, shows the change in side body stripes, or the optional full length side protection strip seen on the Barracuda in the background.

along with variable speed wipers and electric washers.

The most telling difference between that year's E-bodies and the previous year's was the addition of larger bumper overriders with rubber caps front and rear. Introduced because of safety regulations, the overriders were supposed to take and survive an impact at 5mph with no damage. The reinforced bumpers were also moved forward a few inches. On the Challenger this led to the fitting of a silver painted flexible filler strip behind the front bumper. The corporate side markers were fitted on both the Barracuda and Challenger and were raised slightly. The Barracuda had a lower character line than seen on the Challenger, so the new position for the front fender markers touched just below that line. Front and rear spoilers were

169

Dodge Challenger & Plymouth Barracuda

This Plymouth has been heavily modified for the drag strip. The interior has been gutted to a single lightweight bucket seat, a full roll-cage added, and all glass replaced with lighter Perspex. Front and rear spoilers have been added, along with the chute. As one would expect, the engine has also been replaced, in this case by a modified 440 with B1 heads, hooked up to a 727 automatic transmission.

The enormous fibreglass hood and air intake are home-made. All E-bodies remain popular cars to take to the strip. This 'Cuda covers the quarter mile in 9.560 seconds at 136.770mph.

This 1973 base Barracuda is mostly stock except for removal of the large, unsightly front bumper guards and the addition of aftermarket wheels and tires. It is finished in Autumn Bronze Metallic with a white vinyl roof and white interior. There were no significant changes to the Barracuda or 'Cuda styling in 1973 or 1974.

no longer to be found on the factory options list, although the spoilers used in 1971 could be fitted after delivery from the factory to the dealerships.

Inside the car, mildly restyled bucket seats were made from flame-resistant material, again in a bid to meet new safety regulations, and came in black, blue, green or black with white accented vinyl. There were no leather or cloth options this year, and the sunroof was also deleted after the 1972 model year.

The A51 Sport Décor package, introduced in 1972, was still available and offered a 'Cuda sport hood, body stripe in black or white, anodised aluminium wheel lip and body sill moldings. This package was not available on the 'Cuda, only the base Barracuda, although the Light package (A01) was available on all E-bodies and included an ashtray lamp, trunk lamp, glove box lamp, map/courtesy lamp, ignition switch lamp with time delay, time delay instrument panel floodlight, fender mounted

SCALING DOWN – 1972-1974

The rear bumper guards have not been removed, and this rear view shows how large the bumper guards began to grow. They were even deeper in 1974.

turn signals, buzzer and 'headlight on' reminder. The small chrome turn signals mounted on top of each front fender are the obvious giveaway that the Light package was ordered. Also still available was the vinyl roof cover and sunroof option, but the luggage rack for the rear deck lid had to be purchased and fitted through dealers.

There were sixteen body-colors to choose from in 1973 for both E-

This 'Cuda has the 340 engine and looks great in its Light Gunmetal Metallic paint and black vinyl roof, but the billboard sign is not correct for the year and it wears aftermarket chrome wheels. The front and rear rubber bumper guards have been removed. (Courtesy Grahame Bloomfield)

Dodge Challenger & Plymouth Barracuda

bodies, and although both divisions used different names for the enamel paint, they shared the colors and codes. The paints included TX9 Formal Black, JA5 Silver Frost Metallic, EW1 Spinnaker White, HL4 Sahara Beige, JY3 Honey Gold, JY6 Golden Haze Metallic, JY9 Tahitian Gold Metallic, GK6 Autumn Bronze Metallic, JF1 Mist Green, JF8 Forest Green Metallic, HB1 Blue Sky, TB3 Basin Street Blue, GB5 True Blue Metallic, FE5 Rallye Red, GF3 Amber Sherwood Metallic and FY1 Lemon Twist (or Top Banana for Dodge). This last color was the only extra cost paint now left.

As mentioned earlier, the fake air extractors and strobe stripes were part of the Rallye package, with the strobes now available in white as well as black, but the standard Challenger accent decal that followed the contours of the character line could be had in six colors: black, white, light bright blue, medium gold, light green and parchment (beige). The optional full-length, bodyside molding with vinyl insert could only be on the base Challenger without the Rallye pack.

The two remaining engines were the standard 318 V8 with a single Carter BBD two-barrel carburettor that exited through a single exhaust, and the optional 340 V8. Except for a different head casting, the 340 was unchanged from 1972 and still offered 240hp (net) from its 4-barrel carb and dual exhaust setup. The top cover of the pie-tin air filter carried the '340 Four Barrel 340' logo. This engine was optional on the Challenger and 'Cuda, and came with engine call-outs on the side of the performance hoods.

At the end of the year, in a surprise move, Chrysler replaced the 340 with the 360in^3 V8. The new engine featured a shot-peened crankshaft, heavy-duty bearings, high-performance camshaft, chrome-plated exhaust valves, high-load valve springs and surge dampers, double roller timing chain, oil pan windage tray, slip drive fan, and a dual exhaust system. Still fitted with a 4-barrel carb and Hemi Orange filter, those extra twenty cubes from this LA-based engine gave an added 5hp to bring it up to 245hp (net).

With all of these cutbacks, a lack of bold advertising, hikes in fuel costs and an increase in basic price of about $100 per model, it is surprising that both the Barracuda and Challenger made significant increases on sales. Plymouth managed to sell 22,213 E-bodies, 11,587 of which were

An unusual angle for this picture shows off the dummy air intakes on the hood and seams for the vinyl roof, and proves that the car looks great from any angle. (Courtesy Grahame Bloomfield)

Barracudas and 10,626 were 'Cudas. Dodge sold even more with its lone Challenger gaining nearly 6000 additional sales on the 1972 figure to produce a total of 32,596 for 1973. But this was a false peak in a speciality market and few at Chrysler were surprised at what happened next.

1974 THE FINAL CATCH

The year 1974 saw the end of the E-bodies. They entered virtually unchanged and were practically indistinguishable from the previous year's editions.

The car is not just for show, it's built to go. The 'Cuda warms up its tires at Santa Pod Raceway in the heart of England, before ripping down the quarter mile. (Courtesy Tony Oksien)

This factory photo shows the Challenger with part of the Rallye package. Along with a performance hood, buyers could have a blacked-out front grille and lower deck panel, fender scoops with strobe stripes, a Rallye instrument cluster, heavy-duty shock absorbers and suspension, a front sway bar and F70 x 14 tires.

Many companies advertised their products whilst letting you know who they supplied. Many of these were performance items like tires, spark plugs, oil, and as can be seen in this advert from May 1973, gear shifters from B+M.

Dodge Challenger & Plymouth Barracuda

The Challenger went unchanged except for the unsightly but federally mandated front bumper guards. Only one base Challenger remained, with the Rallye becoming an options package, although it was listed in the 1973 Challenger brochure as a model.

There were still sixteen paint colors to choose from, but only one high-impact color – Top Banana. This car is finished in GF3 Light Green Metallic with the optional Green vinyl roof. The roof vinyl could also be had in black, white or gold.

The Barracuda and 'Cuda were still available, both built on the BH23 hardtop body, but still only one Challenger, again, built as a JH23 hardtop. The only way to properly differentiate the models between 1972 and 1974 is by studying the front and rear 'bumperettes' which exponentially increased in size during each consecutive year. The 318 was still the base engine for all three cars while the 340in^3 V8 option had been swapped for the more potent 360 V8. All engines now had electronic ignition as standard, as well as hardened exhaust valve seats for unleaded petrol.

There were some paint color changes, with sixteen hues still available shared by the two divisions, but no extra-cost paints this year. The Plymouth colors were called Golden Haze Metallic JY6, Tahitian Gold Metallic JY9, Sienna Metallic KT5, Dark Moonstone Metallic KL8, Burnished Red Metallic GE7, Frosty Green Metallic KG2, Avocado Gold Metallic KJ6, Deep Sherwood Metallic KG8, Powder Blue KB1, Lucerne Blue Metallic KB5, Golden Fawn KY4, Yellow Blaze KY5, Sahara Beige HL4, Rallye Red FE5, Spinnaker White EW1 and Formal Black TX9.

The oil crisis began on 15 October, 1973, just twenty days after the introduction of the 1974 range from Chrysler, most of which were BIG cars. On that day the members of OAPEC (the Organization of Arab Petroleum Exporting Countries) and OPEC members from Egypt and Syria announced an oil embargo "in response to the US decision to re-supply the Israeli military during the (Yom Kippur) war." OAPEC declared it would no longer ship oil to the United States and other countries if they supported Israel in its conflict with Syria, Egypt and Iraq. It also agreed to use its power over the world price-setting mechanism to effectively raise world oil prices. This of course had an immediate knock-on effect on anything to do with production and transportation. Sales of heavy, full-size, or fast cars were one of the early casualties, with both Challenger and Barracuda production going into full collapse along with their competitors. Early season sales were so poor for the E-bodies that the decision to cease production at the end of the year was brought forward, and in March 1974 the Challenger and Barracuda were quietly dropped, with the last car being produced in late April.

Only 11,734 Barracudas and 'Cudas, and 16,437 Challengers were built before the plug was pulled. There was no fanfare and no big news story when they died. Few mourned their passing. Not surprisingly, sales of the more economical Valiant and Duster increased, taking a staggering 41 per cent of the domestically built compact market in that year. It is also worth remembering that the car that spawned the Barracuda, the lowly Valiant, had outlived its offspring and both of its main rivals, the Chevrolet Corvair and Ford Falcon.

Scaling down – 1972-1974

Challenger and Barracuda Interiors went almost unchanged, too, although the inside of the bucket seats was redesigned for added comfort.

In a surprise move, Chrysler replaced the 340 with a 360 V8 near the end of the 1973 season and continued it into the final year. The LA-based 360 used the same Carter Thermoquad 4-barrel carb seen on the 340, but with a new two-stage, electrically assisted choke. It offered a respectable 245hp (net) and 320lb-ft of torque. It was painted Chrysler Engine Medium Blue and topped by a Hemi Orange single snorkel pie-tin filter. Sadly, few of these cars were sold due to the cessation of production in April 1974, making the last 'Cudas, Barracudas and Challengers amongst the rarest. Only 11,734 Plymouth pony cars were built.

As for the Chrysler E-bodies, today they are the most sought-after muscle cars on Earth, earning astronomical figures at auction – but should they have been dropped in the first place? Was this yet another poorly timed decision by the pencil pushers and accountants that were running Chrysler at the time? Well, in hindsight, one would have to say yes, it was a bad decision. The E-bodies' main competitors, the Camaro and Mustang, both had lean years, but they also responded and bounced back very quickly. By 1976, Camaro production had increased to 182,959, and three years later Chevrolet made 272,631 and had extended the range of models. Chevrolet went on building them through four generations until 2002, and now we have a fifth generation. Its sibling, the Pontiac Firebird, did the same, and it was a similar story for the Mustang – in 1973 its unit production had dropped to 134,867, but by 1979 had rebounded back to 369,936, and of course its success continues.

Dodge and Plymouth never reached the production levels that their stronger competitors achieved, but who is to say that Chrysler couldn't squeeze out more profit from the E-bodies if it had stuck with them? It would have had to spend more money trying to reduce emissions, although this was cured across the corporation in 1977 when it started buying catalytic converters from GM. Also, a next generation was already waiting in the wings, but at that period in time Chrysler needed every dollar it could make and was on the verge of bankruptcy. It stuck to building larger cars that were rushed through with not enough development. The corporation's situation became so precarious in 1974 that it had to shut up shop for four months, laying off staff intermittently over that time. To overcome its shortcomings in the compact and sub-compact market it sold captive imports; foreign cars rebadged as Chryslers. Unfortunately it reused

DODGE CHALLENGER & PLYMOUTH BARRACUDA

Don 'The Snake' Prudhomme moved away from top fuel to his 'Cuda funny car for NHRA competition. He and fellow drag racer Tom 'The Mongoose' McEwen teamed up with toy maker Mattel to race Hot Wheels Barracudas. Both drivers gained wider public attention when Hot Wheels released toy versions of the cars in 1970. Success followed and saw Prudhomme winning the US Nationals in 1973. In 1974 he went on to win the Gatornationals and US nationals in this US Army sponsored 'Cuda.

The Challenger name lost credibility somewhat when Chrysler decided to use it on a sporty version of the Mitsubishi-built Dodge Colt from 1978 to the end of 1984. Although it sold reasonably well, to use such a great name, with such a rich heritage, on a Japanese captive import was a travesty.

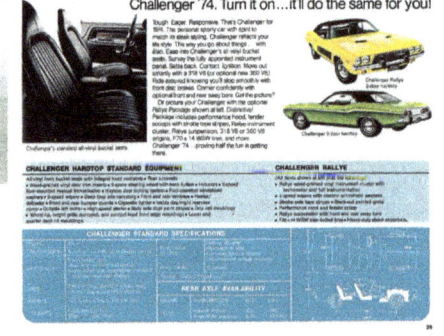

The Challenger for 1974 had been relegated to the back of the Dodge brochure and was sold as a personal sporty car. The Rallye was still touted, but only as an option. Production ceased in the spring of 1974 with only 16,437 built.

the Challenger name on a series of forgettable Mitsubishi-built compacts in the late '70s and early 1980s, but by no means could you call them pony or muscle cars.

The classic Challenger was only built for that short five-year period, leaving us with a limited amount of cars today. As fewer Challengers and Barracudas come up for sale, prices increase, keeping the rarer big-block powered cars for the rich collectors, while even the more mundane (but more driveable) small-block cars achieve high prices at auction. Their limited production time and low sales back in the 70s have helped to make them very special today for owners and enthusiasts alike, so perhaps it wasn't completely the wrong decision in 1974. They became what their designers always wanted them to be: the ultimate pony car.

The one that got away

Chrysler had a four year lead time from design to production, so in early 1969 serious work began on the fourth generation of Barracudas and a new Challenger. Writers have christened these the 1975 cars, because the last E-bodies were built for 1974, but the next generation was in fact due for production in 1972 as 1973 models. For the stylists, morale and enthusiasm was still high, as the hurdles for pony and muscle cars were still around the corner and out of sight. Many sketches were done involving most of the stylists in the Dodge and Plymouth studios, again in competition with each other, to see which studio was going to do the final project. At the same time, work continued on other lines.

From the Plymouth studio two particular designs gained momentum: one from Shunsuke 'Matty' Matsuura, inspired by a theme created by Don Hood, and another from John Samsen. Shunsuke Matsuura had joined the studio in 1964 and had come from Kobe, Japan, via Art Center design college in California, which he was sent to by a

Although this 1968 sketch by John Samsen wasn't specifically for the 1973 E-body program, it shows what stylists wanted to bring us, and how it developed.

The next generation of E-bodies was now in development, and you can see here how Samsen's earlier ideas were taking shape.

Japanese car company. He quickly developed into one of the top stylists in the studio. It soon got to the stage where each studio created two full-size clay models with two different designs on each side. All four of the full-size clay models were placed outside in the stockade, so called because it had a large wooden fence surrounding it, so that everybody could compare the styles.

After many cycles of sketching and modelling, the four clays were whittled down to two, both from the Plymouth studio. One of the Plymouth clay models had a design on one side by John Samsen while the other side had a design by Matty Matsuura, helped by John Herlitz. Both cars had a very European sports car look to them, but Matsuura's had a more muscular aesthetic evolving from the Barracuda, while the Samsen car had more fluidity in its lines. Both designers thought it was important to preserve the ramps found in

Another sketch by Samsen, penned in 1969, this time for a targa top, and similar to a concave design he used back in 1964.

More Samsen images (p179-182). (All images courtesy Brett Snyder)

The one that got away

the shape of the '70 to '74 E-body's front fenders and rear quarters, retaining a certain amount of product heritage. "We struggled to define the fourth generation Barracuda," recalls designer Milt Antonick. "We wanted the car to look more fluid, and yet retain the Barracuda's muscular and aggressive look." At this stage, the clays were rationalised so that each of the two clays had a complete design. Samsen told me, "I was hoping for the rare experience of being responsible for designing a production car pretty much by myself. I used hidden headlamps and no quarter light to keep the smooth lines continuous. We worked separately but of course we saw what the other side was doing and we pooled ideas. My designs were on driver's side A and passenger side B of number 1 model, and Matsuura did passenger side A of the second model, while I think Don Hood did side B. They were to be built on E-body platforms so we stuck to those dimensions."

DODGE CHALLENGER & PLYMOUTH BARRACUDA

Unfortunately for Samsen he didn't get his wish, as the final design was a blend of both his and Matsuura's clays. Vestiges of the previous Barracudas could be seen in the front fender form, but mated to a smoother rear end and full-length rear spoiler. The result infamously became known as 'The Cincinnati Car.'

The final design was created as a full-size model made on a wooden buck overlaid with a 50mm clay outer shell. Modelled by two of Chrysler's best artisans in that medium, Nick O'Shea and Roy Tobias, the final clay surface was coated with a thin plastic membrane called Di-Noc that simulated a reflective paint surface. When gently heated it shrank to the fine lines of the car.

The finished model was a product of refined craftsmanship that was so detailed it was difficult to distinguish from a real car. Using the wooden frame underneath instead of solid clay kept the weight down so that it could be moved around, but even like this the models weighed more than three times what a real car would. This final design was approved from on high and the prototype was transferred to a much lighter fibreglass body, which was then painted silver and detailed to look like a completed car, including a basic interior. In the fall of 1969 the car was taken to a consumer survey group in Cincinnati, OH, which delivered its thoughts on the vehicle. Milt Antonick went with the car, and he told me how the group reacted: "It was a total disaster. They hated

The one that got away

Once the sketching stage had ended, the studios progressed to making clay models. In 1969 when this work was being carried out, the Dodge and Plymouth studios were still separate entities. Dodge created four different designs on two clays and Plymouth did the same. Don Hood left General Motors in 1968 and headed for the Plymouth studio. This is Don Hood's design, still a work in progress.

it. None of the people involved in the survey had an interest in the vehicle and claimed they wanted a small, attractive, fuel efficient car! In other words, a reworked Valiant of sorts. I came back from Cincinnati and knew that was the end for muscle cars. It was one of the saddest days I had at Chrysler."

It was thought at the time by many working at Chrysler that corporate executives had picked Cincinnati because of its reputation for having rather conservative tastes, whereas other areas of the country could have given a more positive result. With its strong European GT styling, this fourth generation Barracuda and its twin Challenger would have instantly made the Camaro and Firebird look dated, almost guaranteeing sales, but Chrysler bosses, as expected, used the Cincinnati result to halt any further plans for major redevelopment of the E-body. Ominously, on the return journey to Detroit, the Cincinnati car fell from a forklift truck while being unloaded, rubbing salt into what were already painful wounds for the design studios. Some minor retouching was done to the prototype and the studio even worked at grafting completely new noses onto an existing Barracuda, but these were also rejected by the top brass.

The stylists knew they were going through the motions and felt this was a huge missed opportunity. With the increase in sales of pony cars built by Chrysler's competitors from 1974-1979, their thoughts were proved correct. The stylists were then tasked with carrying out minor face lift work on the current designs.

Dodge Challenger & Plymouth Barracuda

John Samsen created two slightly different designs on two sides of different Plymouth clays. This is his preferred side (A), which featured a long nose, aerodynamic roof and a full width, moveable rear wing. The quarter-panels ramp up then drop back down toward the rear backlight, while the profile pulls down the greenhouse, making the overall profile lower. Note the twin exhausts coming from the panel just before the rear wheels. The other side was done by John Herlitz. This photo of the Herlitz/Sampson clay was taken in the stockade on 21 April 1969.

This is John's passenger side (B), which looks smoother without the side exhausts.

The One That Got Away

Rear view of the same clay shows Samsen's design had a moving rear spoiler and a clear plastic fairing over the deck for better aerodynamics, which he called a half fastback.

As the seventies progressed, Chrysler's fortunes sank. Poor judgement by the accountants running the company saw diversification into areas other than auto manufacturing, leaving no reserve for product development or for when times got tough. Purchasing other companies around the world and even getting into the real estate business overstretched the corporation. Poorly timed and poorly made cars were having a disastrous effect, too. Safety and emissions legislation also hit Chrysler, harder than it hit the larger Ford or General Motors, causing a downturn in profits.

By 1970, Chrysler was struggling and had to lay off 12,000 workers across North America to help stop the haemorrhaging of money. It wasn't enough. One of the reasons why Chrysler ended up having to pay GM to use its catalytic converters on Mopar cars was because Chrysler hadn't enough resources to develop its own. When Chrysler chairman Lynn Townsend announced his retirement in July of 1975, it was much like the proverbial rat leaving a sinking ship. Replaced by yet another bean counter, John Ricardo, the ship was still afloat but heading for rocks, and the captain was in his cabin, counting pennies, not at the helm, steering through the storm.

In the design studios, morale was at its lowest. Due to the financial cutbacks Chrysler was not putting money into advanced styling projects. Americans were buying the cheaper and more reliable foreign imports. There was a further succession of lay-offs and reorganisation of the studios. Some of the older designers with more expensive salaries or less time to retirement were being purged. Many of the designers responsible for some of the most exciting cars on the planet ended up redundant or drawing minivans and pick-up trucks. It was the end of an era.

All four clays, two from Plymouth, two from the Dodge studio, on show in the stockade. The stockade is what the stylists called the courtyard outside the design studios. It was used for observing the clay models in real light.

This is the infamous 'Cincinnati car,' a compromise design involving styling cues from Matsurra, Antonick, Herlitz and Samsen designs. The consumer review was held in a convention hall in downtown Cincinnati. The clay was silver Di-Noc and had a minimal interior, as the inside had not been developed at that point in time. Milt Antonick was just one of the design staff that went with the car to Ohio and spent some time behind one-way glass, observing the survey people being interviewed. The event was conducted by a research group hired by Chrysler. The people questioned responded negatively to the car in front of them. The clay was based on an E-body-sized frame, and shows how the inner doorskins, side glass, windshield and sill could have been directly carried over from the 1970 E-body in order to save money. In hindsight, there is no way that the front end styling and bumpers would have met the 1973 Federal bumper regulations, but that couldn't have been foreseen back in 1969.

After the car returned from Cincinnati, an effort was made to redesign it. One of Don Hood's aerodynamic designs was grafted onto a production E-body and given two functional air scoops at the front, but this design was also rejected.

Also from Veloce –

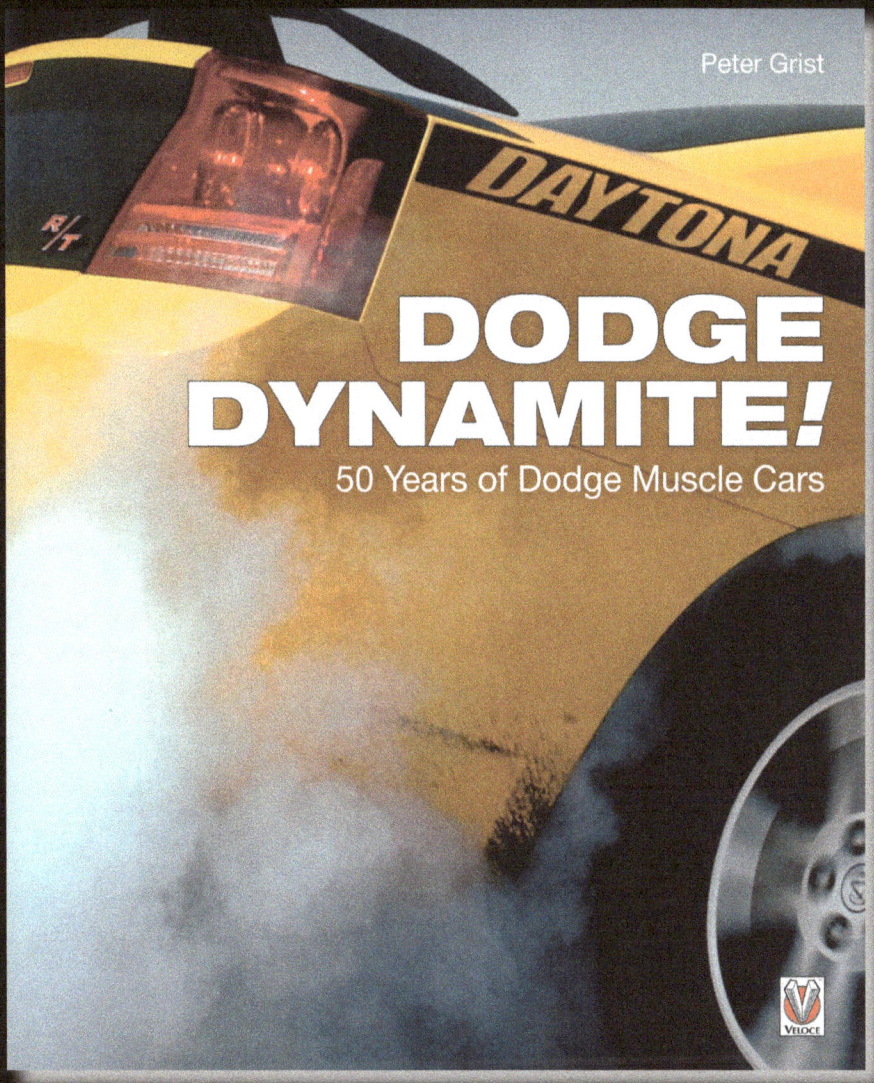

Paperback • 25x20.7cm
• 176 pages • 298 colour and b&w pictures
• ISBN: 978-1-787110-93-9
• UPC: 6-36847-01093-5

This book tells the action-packed story of how Dodge came about and how it became the car to beat. High-octane images show the record breakers, film stars, race cars and concepts, doing what Dodge does best: going faster than anyone else, in superb style.

For more information and price details see our website:
www.velocebooks.com / www.veloce.co.uk

Telephone +44 (0)1305 260068, or email info@veloce.co.uk • Prices subject to change
• Postage and packaging extra

Paperback • 25x20.7cm
• 176 pages • 336 colour and b&w pictures
• ISBN: 978-1-845848-63-7
• UPC: 6-36847-04863-1

Gets inside the character of the man, his strengths and weaknesses, his personal tragedies and his vision of modern transport. Previously unseen works of art and family photos are included. A unique and fascinating insight to a pivotal player in the development of the modern automobile.

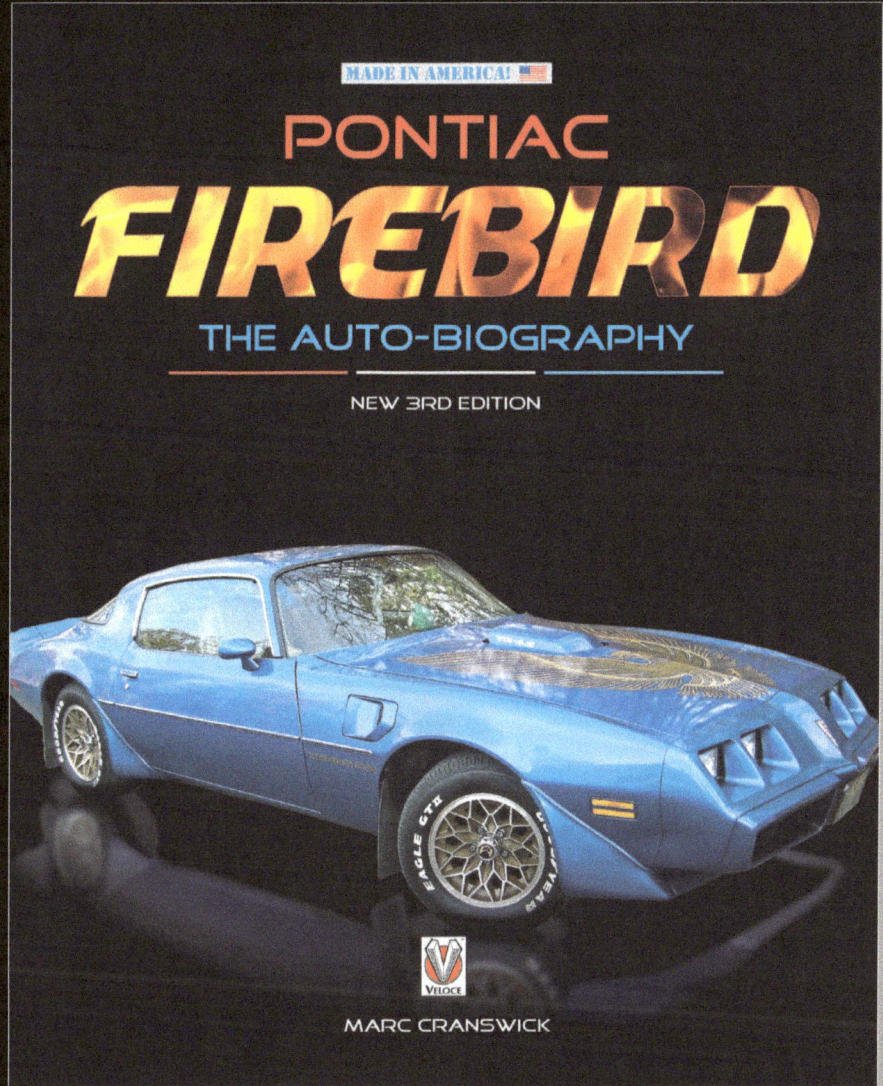

Hardback • 25x20.7cm
• 208 pages • 335 pictures
• ISBN: 978-1-78711-003-8
• UPC: 636847010034

In definitive detail, the story of Pontiac's F-body coupé & convertible during three decades of production & from the height of the personal car/sporty car era of the late '60s, through the fuel crisis/safety-first '70s, '80s renaissance, & '90s indifference. Includes Esprit, SE, Formula & Trans-Am.

www.velocebooks.com / www.veloce.co.uk
Details of all current books • New book news • Special offers

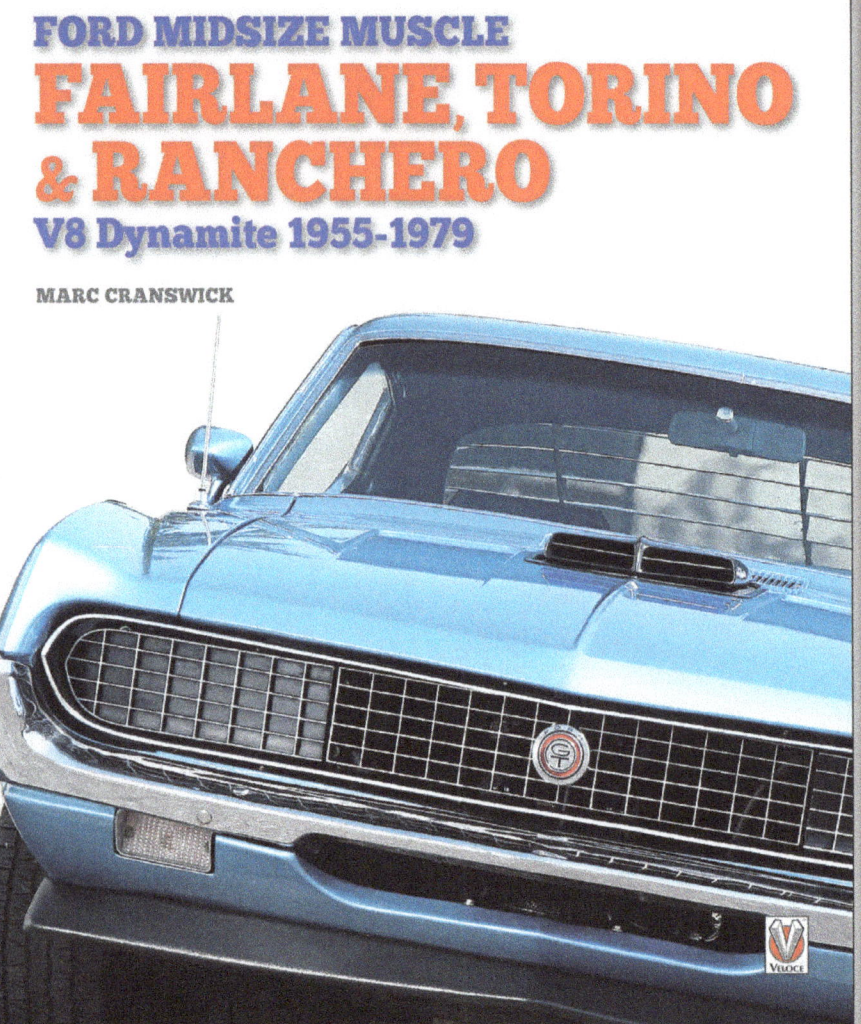

Hardback • 25x20.7cm
• 176 pages • 229 pictures
• ISBN: 978-1-845849-29-0
• UPC: 6-36847-04929-4

The evolution of Ford's family car through the golden era of Detroit, from the Fairlane, to the Gran Torino, to the Ranchero and LTD II ... and beyond!

INDEX

Ackerman, Bob 149-155, 160, 165
Antonick, Milton 13, 17, 31, 32, 40-42, 49, 56, 70, 71, 74-77, 79, 80, 83, 117, 118, 122, 131, 155, 156, 182, 183, 186
Avallito, Jack 75

Backhouse, Frank 78
Baird, Dick 13
Bannister, Tom 13
Barracuda Super Stock 55, 56
Barracuda SX 38, 42
Barris, George 35, 36
Brownlie, William (Bill) 73, 78, 91, 150

Cameron, Carl 73, 75, 78, 81, 91
Carrell, Rick 115
Challenger Pace Car 147-149
Chesebrough, Harry 8, 9
Chevrolet Corvair 6-8, 11
Chrysler Falcon 8, 9
Colbert, Lester 'Tex' 8, 11
Cummins, Dave 12, 13, 16, 26, 40, 41, 74

Diamante Show Car 149

Engle, Elwood 12, 42, 74-77, 80
Exner, Virgil M. Snr 8, 9, 11, 12, 44, 72

Fireball 500 35, 36
Ford, Henry II 11
Ford Mustang 6, 14, 20, 22, 29, 47

Gale, Bob 13, 78, 91
Godshall, Jeff 81, 142, 143
Grotheer, Don 88, 89, 138
Gurney, Dan 123, 124, 127

Hemi Under Glass 32-36

Herlitz, John 37, 38, 40, 41, 74-76, 80, 85, 178, 184, 186
Hood, Don 69, 77, 150, 177, 182 183, 186
Hubbach, Robert 73, 74

Iaccoca, Lee 6

Keller, K.T. 8
Kennets, Jack 13
King, Mack 96
Kopka Don 13

Loda, Peter 13, 74
Lucas, Bill 13

Matsuura, Shunsuke 177, 178, 182, 186
McAdams, Dick 13, 37, 41
McCurry, Robert 81, 82, 150
Mercury Cougar 48

O'Shea, Nick 40, 75, 80, 182

Petty, Lee 11
Posey, Sam 123
Prudhomme, Don 'The Snake' 176

Riggle, Robert (Bob) 32-36
Ritchie, Irving 13, 15, 16, 41
Romeo, Jim 160
RTS 88, 89, 138, 139

Samsen, John (Dick) 13, 16, 18, 23, 27-29, 32, 37, 39-42, 47, 52, 54, 72, 74, 177-182, 184-186
Savage GT 66-68, 70
Savage, Swede 127
Scat Pack 88, 89, 138, 147
Schimmel, Fred 13, 39, 74
Shannon, William 13, 41, 74

Sox & Martin 56, 69, 88, 89
Sturm, Joe 15, 16

Thorley, Gerry 13, 28, 41, 74
Tobias, Roy 40, 75, 80, 182

Valiant 8, 10-12
Voss, Clifford 72, 76

Walling, Neil 13, 74

Washburn, Clint 122
Watson, Dick 150
Weiss, Gene 16

Yazejian, Diran 72, 75
Yellow Jacket Show Car 130

Zaleski, Rick 160

www.ingramcontent.com/pod-product-compliance
Lightning Source LLC
Chambersburg PA
CBHW040738300426
44111CB00026B/2981